Christopher Shakespeare: the man behind the plays

CHRISTOPHER SHAKESPEARE:
the man behind the plays

Malcolm Elliott

Book Guild Publishing

First published in Great Britain in 2016 by
The Book Guild Ltd
9 Priory Business Park
Wistow Road, Kibworth
Leicestershire, LE8 0RX
Freephone: 0800 999 2982
www.bookguild.co.uk
Email: info@bookguild.co.uk
Twitter: @bookguild

Typeset in Baskerville

Printed and bound in Great Britain by
CPI Group (UK) Ltd, Croydon, CR0 4YY

ISBN 978 1 910878 30 9

British Library Cataloguing in Publication Data.
A catalogue record for this book is available from the British Library.

To the memory of Dolly Wraight and the search for truth

Contents

Preface

Professor Alice Hamilton, of the University of Winnipeg, was staying in Leicester as she did every year during the summer vacation, pursuing her research into the medieval mystery plays. She had a hunch that she might find reference to a cycle of plays among the voluminous records of the guilds of the medieval town. It was the day in 1982 when British soldiers recaptured the Falkland Islands, and we were sauntering over what was then thought to be the site of the Battle of Bosworth. We were unaware, then, that the battle had actually taken place on Ambion Hill, some two miles west of King Dickon's Well, and it would be another three decades before King Richard III's body was rediscovered, under a car park in the middle of Leicester.

Perhaps it was the memory of Henry V's speech on the eve of Agincourt that prompted Alice to remark: 'It has always astounded me that England should have produced not one, but two men of exceptional genius at the very same time.'

'You mean Shakespeare,' I said, 'but who else?'.

'Why Marlowe, of course, Marlowe,' she replied.

For my benefit, Alice elaborated on Marlowe's talents, his command of blank verse, his facility in metaphor and his astonishing output for a man still in his twenties when he died. Her panegyric took me back to an English lesson in school when a young Oxford graduate, on teaching practice, introduced us to the authorship controversy. He was researching the religious views of William Shakespeare, and evidently had his doubts about the true identity of the man responsible for the thirty-six plays attributed to Shakespeare.

The class was not impressed when he told us about the credentials of various noble contenders – the Earl of Oxford, or of Derby, or Rutland or Francis Bacon – but the son of a Canterbury shoemaker, who won a scholarship to Cambridge, and who was already the author of half a dozen plays, was a different matter. Surely he was the obvious choice for the bardic throne? There was palpable disappointment when we learned that Marlowe could not have written anything after 1593, because he was stabbed to death in a brawl at Deptford. Whoever wrote the works of Shakespeare, it could not have been Christopher Marlowe.

I make no claim to original research or for the material used in this book. It is based very largely on the pioneering work of A.D. Wraight and Peter Farey who examined the evidence on Marlowe's supposed death, in 1593, and found it utterly unconvincing. Mrs Wraight would have said how much she and all other Marlowe scholars were building on the pioneering work of Dr Leslie Hotson, who revealed the implausibility of the proceedings of the coroner's court that met following the supposed death at Deptford. Hotson also wrote a book called *The First Night of Twelfth Night* – a fascinating detective story and a major contribution to our knowledge of the Shakespearean theatre. We shall return to this later.

Mrs Wraight searched the sonnets for clues as to Marlowe's 'afterlife' and made further assumptions about his identity in *New Evidence*. But her belief that Marlowe went under the name of M. Le Doux and lived at Burley-on-the-Hill in Rutland has been disproved by Geoffrey Caveney and Peter Farey. For much of the material relating to Marlowe's early life and his literary output, I am indebted to the splendid work by Professor Park Honan, *Christopher Marlowe: Poet and Spy*. I am also heavily indebted to Daryl Pinksen for his superb book *Marlowe's Ghost*, which covers all aspects of the downfall and subsequent career of Marlowe, and, finally, I am indebted to the wonderful detective work of the late Richard Paul Roe who, impressed by the number of Italian plays and the topographical details mentioned in them, devoted many years to verifying the accuracy of Shakespeare's Italian references. His work finally resulted in a book, *The Shakespeare Guide to Italy*, published in 2011, the year after his death, and my debt to him will be apparent to anyone reading this book. His thoroughness and pertinacity were astounding. He made it abundantly clear that whoever wrote the plays must have had detailed knowledge of, and personal acquaintance with, the urban life of Italy.

I would also like to express my thanks to my daughter Rebecca Poles, for her invaluable help in compiling the index and in additional proof-reading. Anything incorrect remaining is mine and mine alone.

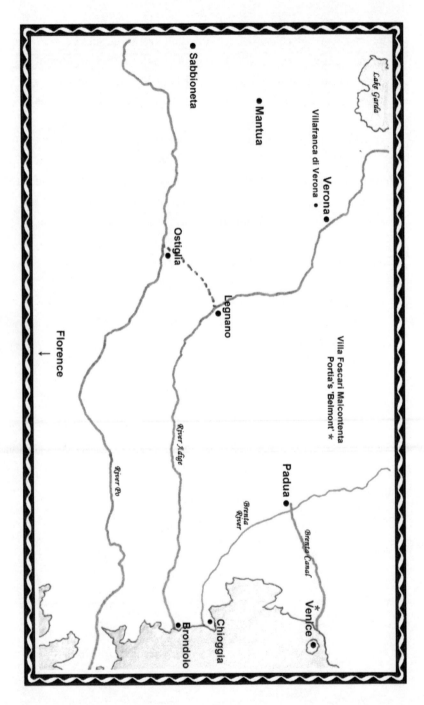

1

The Cobbler's Son

Christopher Marlowe was born in Canterbury and christened on 26 February 1564, just two months before William Shakespeare. His mother was a native of Dover and his father, John Marley, came from the village of Ospringe, just a few miles west of Canterbury. He was a cobbler and good enough to become warden of the Guild of Shoemakers. They had a house in George Street a few yards from St George's church, where Christopher was baptised. John made a decent living as a cobbler, but he was never flush with money and it may be that he was helped occasionally by a wealthy benefactor, Sir Roger Manwood, who became Baron of the Exchequer. Marlowe later composed elegiac verses to his memory, perhaps by way of acknowledging the family's debt to him.

It was a family of four younger sisters until, when he was 12 years old, he had a brother, Thomas, but the age gap was too great for any close intimacy between them. Two other boy babies died in infancy. Of his four sisters, the first two probably idolised Christopher and contributed to a happy domestic environment as he was growing up. The later pair of sisters turned out to be somewhat wayward and foul-mouthed. Both appear in the court records for breaking the Queen's peace, but by this time their older brother had long left Canterbury.

The place was less prosperous than it had been under the

old religion, when thousands of pilgrims flocked to worship at the shrine of Thomas Becket, but it was still a vibrant city, with all kinds of tradesmen and craftsmen at work within its walls. And the great cathedral provided plenty of pomp and pageantry for the gaze of small boys, living within the walls of the city.

Just outside the town were the ruins of another great church in the Abbey of St Augustine. We can imagine the young Christopher wandering among the dilapidated cloisters and ecclesiastical buildings, trying to comprehend the enormity of the changes in religious and social life that had swept over England in the previous half century. He would have been told of the execution and burning of Friar Stone in a field outside Canterbury in 1539, and of the plundering of Becket's shrine. Two heavy trunk-loads of precious jewels and plate were carried away by eight men, staggering under their weight.

Marlowe would also have heard of the 41 Protestant martyrs burned, just outside Canterbury's walls, in 1556, as Mary Tudor tried to restore the faith of her mother. But there was no going back, as the dilapidated priory demonstrated. Now, in the hands of its secular owner, the old roof over the nave and chancel was replaced by a new one, supported by red brick where the stonework had been taken away. Other parts of the complex remained as ghostly ruins, doubtless grazed by sheep and cattle.

As a boy, Marlowe would also have been aware of the great influx of foreigners that came across the Channel to Dover, after the massacre of St Bartholomew's Eve, in 1572, when French Catholics rounded on their Protestant neighbours in an horrific orgy of butchery. Some Huguenot refugees settled in the town, and Marlowe might well have heard their stories. Travellers and visitors came through the east gate, not far from his home, bringing an awareness of the world beyond, firing his youthful imagination. He would also have seen the Queen when she visited the town, to stay with Archbishop Parker in September 1573, surrounded by her enormous retinue of servants, and he probably sang High Mass to her in the cathedral.

Proximity to the parish church did not bring access to religious education, for the pastor at St George's church, William Sweeting, was virtually illiterate and had to find others to preach the occasional sermon. But he had a son, Leonard, with whom Christopher went to school. The boys may have had their first tutoring at a petty school, held in a half empty shop, and run by a clerk, who would have taught them to read and learn the alphabet.

Marlowe possibly gained a place in the Cathedral Choir School at the age of 9, enabling him to participate in the music that filled the church for the Queen's visit to Archbishop Parker. At 14, he gained a scholarship to the King's School where he learned Latin and Greek, religion and history. He would have been encouraged to write verses and to perform plays in Latin. It is very likely that he was allowed to make use of the library of Dr Gresshop, the headmaster, under whom he sat for at least three terms in 1579. Gresshop's library was renowned as one of the greatest in England, with over 350 volumes. Professor Honan tells us that among other volumes it contained were: Calvin's letters and Geneva catechism, French erotic poems, the plays of Aristophanes, Terence and Plautus, the English play, *Gorboduc*, and modern historical works.

It was probably in the library of Dr Gresshop that Marlowe gained his abiding love of the classics. According to Professor Honan, 'Marlowe was dazzled by the classics. Nothing in his imaginative life was to be the same again, and it may be that no discovery he made, and no love he ever felt, affected his mind and feelings so terribly, so unsettlingly as the writers of ancient Rome.' 'Sooner or later,' says Professor Honan, 'he also found a sanity in the pagan viewpoints of Horace, Ovid and Virgil, as they appealed to his rational sense; nobody ever raised in England, perhaps, has been more affected by the classics of Rome' (Honan 52). From these writers he drew the material for his early play, *Dido, Queen of Carthage*, as well as his translations of Ovid's *Amores*, and the verse drama of *Hero and Leander*.

John C. Baker believes that Marlowe may have been part author of a satirical work called *Timon*, a trivial but funny school play that parodies the voyage of Sir Francis Drake in circumnavigating the globe. Drake had family ties in Kent and one of his younger brothers appears to have been a scholar at the King's School. One character in the play, a 'lying traveller' is made to fly round the world in a wooden flying machine. The journey takes him three years, six months and four days, exactly the length of Drake's voyage.

There are elements of farce in the play but also of tragedy, and Professor Honan gives the following instance of what certainly sounds like Marlowe's poetry, in which Timon rages at the perfidy of his erstwhile friends:

> Fire water sworde confounde yee, let the crowes
> Feede on your peckt out entrailes, and your bones
> Wante a sepulchre: worthy oh worthy yee
> That thus have, falsifi'd your faith to mee.
> To dwell in Phlegeton. rushe on me heav'n
> Soe that on them it rushe, mount Caucasus
> Fall on my shoulders, soe on them it fall
> Paine I respecte not: O holy Justice
> If thou inheritte heav'n descende at once
> Ev'n all at once unto a wretches hands
> Make mee an Arbiter of Ghosts in Hell

That when they shall with an unhappy pace
Descende the silent house of Erebus
They may feele paines that never tongue can tell.

Honan 66

The poetry has a distinctly Marlovian ring and Professor Honan comments, 'If his own writing is here, what we have is a young Marlowe trapped in amber.' It may well have inspired him to write the mature work, *Timon of Athens*, which is now recognised, by authorities like the American scholar James C. Bulman, as the work of Marlowe rather than of William Shakespeare.

Playwriting and acting were much more important to the curriculum in Marlowe's time than ever before or since. The boys were encouraged to stage plays with a far greater licence than that which could be obtained in the world of public theatre. 'A "lewde play" was pounced on in the city, but city authorities left the school alone,' says Professor Honan, and he gives the example of works by John Bale, a Canterbury canon who died in 1563. Known as 'Bilious Bale', he 'turned into a fierce mocker of Rome', whose 'spirit of iconoclasm would have kept the boys awake'. Honan gives a rather choice example of Bale's irreverent wit. In his *King Johan*, when corrupt friends bear on stage their bulky master, Sedition, the latter is pleased:

'Yea, thus it should be', cries Sedition from a lofty perch,
'Marry, now I am aloft
I will beshit you all if ye set me not down soft.'

Honan 63

Before Archbishop Parker died in 1575, he created three endowments, including one scholarship for a boy who was a native of Canterbury and a scholar at the King's School.

It might have been made for Marlowe. In addition to facility in Latin, he had to be able to sight read and sing plainsong. Faced with a dearth of parish priests, this was one way in which the archbishop might hope to gain new entrants into the priesthood, as the successful scholars were expected to enter the Church as ministers. Thus Christopher Marlowe duly entered Corpus Christi College, Cambridge, in December 1580.

2

Cambridge Scholar and Spy

Marlowe was still only 16 when he entered Corpus Christi, three weeks before Christmas. He was lodged in a converted storehouse in part of what is today called the Old Court. Unlike most of the undergraduate rooms, it had a fireplace and chimney, and he would have had his own desk at which to study. He had a bursary of £3.6s.8d per annum and received a regulation dark-coloured gown with a hood. Only 'sad colours' were allowed. Scholars were not allowed to wear any other garb and there were stringent regulations as to exactly what the gowns were made of and how they were to be worn. They had a new one every Christmas.

His first four years were spent in diligent study, during which time he wrote his first major dramatic works as well as translating the poems of Lucan and Ovid. His first essay into drama, if we discount the school play *Timon*, was probably *The True History of George Scanderbeg*, about a heroic Albanian prince who fought against the Turks, driving them out of his land and restoring it to Christianity. The text has been lost, but it is clearly the sort of story that appealed to the young Marlowe, still intending to take holy orders. His next play, which has survived, was *Dido, Queen of Carthage*, based on Virgil's *Aeneid*. The play is full of delightful poetry, written in blank verse. It lacks the development of character and dramatic force that mark his later work, but it is an astounding first essay into full-length drama. Take the following passage, from the end of Act Two, as an example of Marlowe's skill with dramatic dialogue. Dido asks what became of Helen:

Dido	But how scaped Helen, she that caused this war?
Aeneas	Achates, speak; sorrow hath tired me quite.
Achates	What happened to the Queen we cannot show:
	We hear they led her captive into Greece;
	As for Aeneas, he swum quickly back,
	And Helena betrayed Deiphobus,
	Her lover after Alexander died,
	And so was reconciled to Menelaus.
Dido	O had that 'ticing strumpet ne'er been born!'

Dido, Queen of Carthage, Act II

Marlowe also translated Lucan's *Pharsalia*, about the war between Pompey and Caesar, in blank verse and he translated Ovid's *Amores* into rhyming couplets. All this afforded plentiful material for future use and made the writing of verse second nature to him.

It is worth noting the erotic nature of Ovid's work in the light of accusations of homosexuality that are often made against Marlowe. Ovid's hero seduces Corinna whom he describes thus:

How apt her breasts were to be pressed by me.
How smooth a belly under her waist saw I?
How large a leg, and what a lusty thigh?
To leave the rest, all liked me passing well,
I clinged her naked body, down she fell.
Judge you the rest: being tired she bade me kiss;
Jove send me more such afternoons as this.

The young lover talks to his aberrant organ for not behaving as he wants, berating it for limpness when 'like one dead it lay'. He describes how Corinna,

> did not disdain a whit
> To take it in her hand and play with it,
> But when she saw it would by no means stand,
> But still drooped down, regarding not her hand,
> 'Why mock'st thou me,' she cried, 'or being ill,
> Who bade thee lie down here against thy will?'
>
> Ovid, *Elegies*, IV, lines 20–6 and III, vi, lines 73–8

Not surprisingly, when a translation appeared in print after Marlowe's supposed death, it was promptly banned by the Church authorities and publicly burned.

A bachelor's degree depended largely on the ability to defend logical propositions, with fellow students providing the contrary arguments. It is the kind of reasoning espoused by Faustus in Marlowe's play about the over-confident doctor.

By Easter 1584, Marlowe had completed his baccalaureate, but at this point he began to absent himself from the university. He had come to the notice of Sir Francis Walsingham, the Queen's spymaster, who was always on the lookout for promising young men to serve their country abroad. He therefore dropped out of his studies for some months and may have attended the Catholic seminary at Rheims, to where the English college removed itself from Douai in 1578. It was widely known as the centre of Catholic evangelism, where young men were trained to keep alive Catholicism in England, crossing the Channel in disguise in order to minister to the faithful, wherever households remained true to the religion of Rome. Theirs was a highly dangerous mission, hiding in priest holes and suffering horrendous punishment if they were betrayed and caught.

It is possible that, while abroad, Marlowe was able to pass on information that led to the unveiling of the Babbington plot to murder Elizabeth. These were the years leading to the war with Spain, and he may also have been gathering intelligence about the impending Spanish invasion. John Bakeless makes out a strong case for Marlowe having been in France gaining knowledge of the build-up of Spanish forces only two days before the Armada was sighted off the English coast.

When Christopher Marlowe returned to Cambridge, there were those who questioned the reason for his long absence abroad, suspecting that he might have defected to Rome. Some of the dons were therefore reluctant to confer on him the degree of Master of Arts. News of this academic obstacle came to the ears of the Privy Council with the result that a letter put the reluctant dons firmly in their place. Elizabeth and her chief ministers were evidently aware of Christopher Marlowe and quite definitely on his side:

> Whereas it was reported that Christopher Marlowe was determined to have gone beyond the seas to Rheims and there to remain, their lordships thought it good to certify that he had no such intent, but that in all his actions he had behaved himself orderly and discretely whereby he had done her Majesty good service, and deserved to be rewarded for his faithful dealing: their Lordships' request was that the rumour thereof should be allayed by all possible means, and that he should be furthered in the degree he was to take this next Commencement: because it was not her

Majesty's pleasure that anyone employed as he had been in matters touching the benefit of his country should be defamed by those that are ignorant in the affairs he went about.

The document is signed by Archbishop Whitgift; Sir Christopher Hatton, the Lord Chancellor; Lord Burghley, the Lord Treasurer; Lord Hunsdon, the Lord Chamberlain, and Sir James Croft as Mr Comptroller. It was dated 29 June 1587, five months after the execution of Mary Stuart.

At about this time Marlowe may have had his portrait painted as a parting gift to his old college. The putative Marlowe portrait was discovered in 1952 by an undergraduate living in the Old Court. Alterations were being made to the buildings and workmen had thrown out two oak planks, which they had found under an old gas fire and dumped in a skip. The wooden planks were rescued by Mr Hall, the undergraduate, who had intended to build a storage unit for his hi-fi. He saw what looked like a painting and had the planks examined by a number of experts. After being photographed the portrait was renovated and hung in Corpus Christi hall as probably that of Christopher Marlowe.

The portrait shows a young man aged 22, and is inscribed with the motto: '*Quod me nutrit me destruit*' – 'what nourishes me, destroys me'. It calls to mind the words of Sonnet 73, which includes almost the same words and seems to refer to sudden loss of prestige and honour, and, incidentally, there may be a reference to the 'bare ruined choirs' of the Abbey of St Augustine:

That time of year thou mayst in me behold
When yellow leaves, or none, or few do hang
Upon those boughs which shake against the cold,

Bare ruined choirs, where late the sweet birds sang.
In me thou seest the twilight of such day
As after sunset fadeth in the West,
Which by and by black night doth take away,
Death's second self that seals up all in rest.
In me thou seest the glowing of such fire
That on the ashes of his youth doth lie,
As the death-bed, whereon it must expire,
Consum'd with that which it was nourished by.
   This thou perceiv'st, which makes thy love
   more strong
   To love that well, which thou must leave
   ere long.

The portrait is dated 1585 after he had been awarded his BA. Having obtained his MA he was free to indulge his passion for writing and he set about completing his first runaway success in *Tamburlaine*. It was such a triumph that he wrote a sequel almost immediately. *Tamburlaine* tells the story of the ruthless conqueror of Asia, who defeated the Turks and imposed his will on every power he encountered. His sons, Celebinus and Amyras, promise to follow his example in being 'the scourge and terror of the world'. Tamburlaine replies with a blistering testimony to his own ruthless philosophy:

For he shall wear the crown of Persia
Whose head hath deepest scars, whose breast
most wounds,
Which being wroth sends lightning from his
eyes,
And in the furrows of his frowning brows
Harbours revenge, war, death and cruelty;
For in a field, whose superficies

Is covered with a liquid purple veil
And sprinkled with the brains of slaughtered
men,
My royal chair of state shall be advanced;
And he that means to place himself therein
Must armed wade up to the chin in blood.

Tamburlaine II, Act I, sc. iii, lines 71–84

Perhaps his most horrific act occurs in Part II, where he kills his son for failing to emulate his own addiction to battle. He is at his most bombastic in Act IV, Scene iii, where he comes on stage in a chariot drawn by two kings of Asia with bits in their mouths, Tamburlaine scourging them with a whip:

'Holla, ye pampered jades of Asia!
What can ye draw but twenty miles a day,
And have so proud a chariot at your heels,
And such a coachman as great Tamburlaine? ...

Tamburlaine continues to bait them promising:

'To make you fierce, and fit my appetite,
You shall be fed with flesh as raw as blood
And drink in pails the strongest muscadel;
If you can live with it, then live and draw
My chariot swifter than the racking clouds;
If not, then die like beasts, and fit for nought
But perches for the black and fatal ravens.

Yet Tamburlaine demonstrates his ability to express the most sublime poetry, inviting Zenocrate, daughter of the Soldan of Egypt, to sit on the Turkish throne:

13

Zenocrate, the lovliest maid alive,
Fairer than rocks of pearl and precious stone,
The only paragon of Tamburlaine,
Whose eyes are brighter than the lamps of heaven,
And speech more pleasant than sweet harmony;
That with thy looks can clear the darkened sky
And calm the rage of thund'ring Jupiter:
Sit down by her, adorned with my crown,
As if thou wert the empress of the world.'

Tamburlaine I, Act III, sc. iii, lines 116–25

The force of Marlowe's poetry and his ability to create dramatic tension save the plays from being too predictable. Tamburlaine was so successful that touring companies took it round England. The good citizens of Shrewsbury were so entranced by the play that several named their boy children Tamburlaine.

It is probable that Marlowe not only wrote *Tamburlaine* but had a hand in its production, striking up a friendship with the leading actor, Edward Alleyn. He was the son-in-law of Philip Henslow, the impresario, whose diary provides such a rich source of information for the whole theatrical world of the time. Alleyn is almost certainly the 'Shake-scene' against whom Robert Greene inveighed in his 'Groatsworth of Wit' (1592). Orthodox Shakespearean scholars have often seized on this reference as evidence pertaining to Shakespeare's 'lost years', but the case for its being aimed at Alleyn has been strongly argued by Mrs Wraight in her book, *Christopher Marlowe and Edward Alleyn* (1993).

Marlowe's next play, *The Massacre at Paris*, was based on the appalling slaughter of Protestant citizens, on St Bartholomew's Eve, 20 years earlier. Marlowe must have met and heard stories of Huguenot refugees while he was a boy in Canterbury. The fanaticism and savagery of the attacks is hard to credit in a civilised country, though perhaps it is no more deplorable than the ethnic cleansing of our own day. The debacle began with the shooting of Admiral Coligny on 22 August 1572. At this, the duc d'Anjou and his mother, Catherine de Medici, seized the opportunity to liquidate the entire Protestant community. Two or three thousand Huguenots died in less than a week, and a further 10,000 or 15,000 more died in the provinces. The scale of the slaughter pales perhaps only in an age that has witnessed the horrors of the gas chambers. We seek in vain to fathom the causes of man's inhumanity to man, but Professor Honan says that 'Marlowe is probably the first English writer to look into factors which, among other causes, contributed to the massacre of the Huguenots as to the twentieth century's Holocaust' (274).

Even as he describes the thrusting of Admiral Coligny's body into the river, Marlowe's comic genius betrays itself. In a passage referring to the medieval notion of airborne transmission of disease, the so-called miasmatic theory, two men discuss what's to be done with the corpse:

One   Now, sirrah, what shall we do with the Admiral?
Two   Why let's burn him for a heretic.
One   Oh no, his body will infect the fire, and the fire the air, and so we shall be poisoned with him.
Two   What shall we do then?
One   Let's throw him into the river.
Two   O, 'twill corrupt the water, and the water the fish, and by the fish ourselves, when we eat them.

The Massacre at Paris, Act I, sc. XI, lines 1–8

They decide instead to leave him hanging on a tree, whereupon Queen Catherine de Medici enters with the Duke of Guise:

'Now, Madam, how like you our lusty Admiral?' he asks the Queen. 'Believe me, Guise', she replies:

> he becomes the place so well
> As I could long ere this have wished him there.
> But come, let's walk aside; th'air's not very sweet.
>
> ibid., 13–16

Guise instead suggests that they throw him in a ditch and he then turns to the matter of how to murder the remaining Huguenots. The Queen urges him to kill them immediately, lest they recover and disperse throughout France, when: 'It will be hard for us to work their deaths'. With these words she dismisses him: 'Be gone, delay no time, sweet Guise.' His reply sounds even more unfeeling: 'Madam, I go as whirlwinds rage before a storm' (ibid., 27–29).

The Massacre at Paris was probably the last Marlowe wrote before his appointment with destiny at Deptford. He had published *Hero and Leander* early in 1593, and was probably working on *Venus and Adonis* at the same time. In the early years of the decade, he was also working on the Henrician cycle, *Henry VI* parts one, two and three, and on *Edward II* and *III*.

Shakespearean scholars have differed, over the years, as to whether the history plays belong to Marlowe, or to Shakespeare. There seems every reason to think that they are by the same hand, with a degree of extra polish in the later plays, and a facility that becomes even more apparent as Marlowe completed the cycle with *Henry V* and *Henry IV* parts one and two.

It is probable that Marlowe's next dramatic venture after *Tamburlaine* was *Edward III*, the authorship of which is disputed. Once again, the indefatigable Mrs Wraight has produced strong evidence that it belongs to Marlowe. At the same time he was engaged in writing another early play based on the death of a local citizen, who was murdered by his wife, *Arden of Faversham*. Then, in the same year, 1589, he produced two of his great tragedies, *The Jew of Malta* and *Dr Faustus*. Both of these were written for Alleyn's company, The Lord Admiral's Men, as were *The Massacre at Paris*, *Edward II* and the second part of *Henry VI*, two years later.

The character of Dr Faustus is sometimes said to be based upon Dr Dee of Queen Elizabeth's court, but in fact he was a German chemist who met his end in an alchemic experiment, at Stauffen, in around 1540. Marlowe's play gives the lie to the charge that he could not handle comedy in the way that Shakespeare did. The main plot concerns Faustus and his pact with the devil, but alongside the intellectual struggles of the learned doctor, we meet his irreverent and cheerfully amoral servant Wagner.

Wagner enjoys making fun of the scholars who seek out Faustus. When they ask where he is to be found, Wagner delivers a long irrelevant piece of nonsense before telling them: 'Truly my dear brethren, my master is within at dinner with Valdes and Cornelius, as this wine, if it could speak, would inform your worships. And so, the Lord bless you, preserve you, and keep you, my dear brethren' (*Dr Faustus*, 1616 text, Act I, sc. ii, 25–29). When Wagner meets the clown, Robin, he is treated to some of his own medicine. After Wagner addresses him as 'sirrah boy', Robin retorts with: '"Boy"! O, disgrace to my person! Zounds, "boy" in your face – you have seen many boys with beards, I am sure.' The banter continues and Wagner offers to employ Robin as his servant 'in beaten silk and stavesacre'. 'Stavesacre?' replies Robin, 'That's good to kill vermin. Then belike if I serve you I shall be lousy' (ibid., Act I, sc. iv, 1–18).

Robin also meets his match in the hostess of an inn. He brags to a fellow customer that he owes 18 pence to the woman,

'But say nothing. See if she hath forgotten me.' He greets her with the casual remark: 'I hope my score stands still', to which she replies: 'Ay, there's no doubt of that, for me thinks you make no haste to wipe it out.' There follows a further passage in which a carter gives a long rambling account of how Faustus duped him into selling some hay 'to eat'. 'Now, sir, I thinking that a little would serve his turn, bade him take as much as he would for three farthings. So he presently gave me my money and fell to eating; and as I am a cursen man, he never left eating till he had eaten up all my load of hay' (ibid., Act IV, sc. v, 112–32). Scenes like this employ the sort of lowlife alehouse humour that contrasts with the serious main theme of the play. They remind one of the tavern scenes in *Henry IV* or the porter in *Macbeth*, or the gravedigger in *Hamlet*.

During the course of the last century, the trilogy of *Henry VI* plays was ascribed to both Marlowe and Shakespeare, a fact which lends credence to our claim that they were one and the same. While the Henrician cycle of plays is now generally attributed to Shakespeare, they were, in the early twentieth century, seen as the work of Marlowe. In 1912, Professor C.F. Tucker Brooke, of Yale University, wrote an article on 'The Authorship of the Second and Third Parts of *King Henry VI*'. He found significant similarities of language and ideas between *The First Part of the Contention of the Two Famous Houses of York and Lancaster*, otherwise known as Henry VI part two, and *The True Tragedy of Richard Duke of York and the Good King Henry the Sixth*, otherwise known as *Henry VI* part three, and other works of Marlowe such as *Edward II* and *The Massacre at Paris*. For example, in *The Contention* we have, in Act II, lines 49–50:

But still must be protected like a child,
And governed by that ambitious Duke.

While, in *Edward II* we have:

> As though your highness were a schoolboy still,
> And must be governed like a child.

Or, to take one other example, in *The Contention*, we have:

> Even to my death for I have lived too long.

And in *Edward II*, Marlowe wrote:

> Nay, to my death, for too long have I lived.

Parallels between the *True Tragedy* and *The Massacre at Paris* and *Edward II* are even more numerous, for example, in the *True Tragedy*, we have:

> Sweet duke of Yorke, our prop to lean upon,
> Now thou art gone there is no hope for us.

In the *Massacre* we have:

> Sweet Duke of Guise, our prop to lean upon,
> Now though art dead, heere is no stay for us.

Tucker Brooke gives 28 such examples of similar phrasing. Likewise Professor Alison Gaw, in an article for the University of Southern California in 1926, discussed 'The Origin and Development of the first part of Henry VI in Relation to Shakespeare, Marlowe, Peele and Greene'. He found a close relation between this play and Marlowe's *Massacre at Paris* and *Edward II* as well as the later parts of *Henry VI*.

It seems probable that *Edward II* was written after *Edward*

III and after the three parts of *Henry VI*, making it one of the last plays generally attributed to Marlowe. It is regarded by many as his masterpiece and is often compared to the later plays of Shakespeare. It is also adduced as evidence of his homosexuality, but there is no more reason to suspect Marlowe of the vices indulged in by his characters than to charge Shakespeare with multiple murder and horrific deeds of mutilation, as in *King John* or *Lear*. Of course, he had to portray the sexual relationship with Gaveston, because it was central to the accusations made against the King, and to his obloquy in the popular imagination, but Marlowe can hardly be said to endorse the regal obsession. The relationship of the male lovers is hardly rewarded with ultimate satisfaction; Gaveston is butchered to death by a bunch of noble thugs and Edward dies in the most horrendous act of anal penetration imaginable.

Almost as important to the plot is the plight of Queen Isabella, trying to be loyal to her royal spouse, yet increasingly pushed out of his affections by his court favourite:

> In vain I look for love at Edward's hand,
> Whose eyes are fixed on none but Gaveston.
>
> Act II, sc. iv, lines 61–62

There is little doubt where Marlowe's sympathies lie. When Isabella asks Edward 'Whither goes my lord?' he replies brusquely: 'Fawn not on me, French strumpet; get thee gone.' She replies with the question: 'On whom but my husband should I fawn?' Gaveston then intervenes, accusing her of having an affair with Mortimer, to which she answers:

> In saying this, thou wrongst, me Gaveston.
> Is't not enough that thou corrupts my lord.

And art a bawd to his affections,
But thou must call mine honour thus in question?

                                    Act I, sc. iv, lines 143–52

Of all Marlowe's plays, this is the one that most clearly belongs to the Shakespearean canon. It forms the logical starting point for the whole cycle of historical plays relating to the history of England. *King John* takes the story back nearly two centuries earlier, but Marlowe was clearly more interested in the conflicts between York and Lancaster, the so-called 'Wars of the Roses', that had their origin in the seizure of the Crown from Richard II in 1399. The fate of Edward II was a significant precursor to that event. Both kings met their downfall as a result of indulging in homoerotic dalliance with court favourites. One wonders why the playwright never tackled the long reign of Henry III, but possibly the deposition of the king, by Simon de Montfort, would have made it too sensitive a subject to put before the public in Elizabeth's jittery last decade.

In addition to this remarkable output of dramatic works, Marlowe also wrote poetry, most of which has disappeared. His verse drama, *Hero and Leander*, was written in about 1593 but was published in 1598 after his supposed death, with an ending supplied by George Chapman. *Venus and Adonis*, which burst onto the literary world in July 1593, just after the 'death' at Deptford, under the name of William Shakespeare, is clearly the work of the classical scholar, Marlowe, rather than the previously unheard-of and relatively uneducated jobbing actor from Stratford. Authors did not always attach their names to their works, and *Venus and Adonis* had, in fact, been registered anonymously in April 1593.

It must be remembered that actors were not generally men of polish and refinement. According to Stephen Greenblatt: 'Actors were classified officially as vagabonds; they practised a trade that was routinely stigmatised and despised. As "masterless men" – men without a home of their own or an honest job or an attachment to someone else's home – they could be arrested, whipped, put in the stocks, and branded. (This is why they described themselves legally as the servants of aristocrats or as guild members.)' (Greenblatt, *Will in the World*, 74). Marlowe's early plays were staged by Lord Strange's company. They changed their name to Lord Derby's Men when Ferdinand Stanley, Lord Strange, became Earl of Derby. Then, when he died in April 1594, they were taken under the patronage of Lord Hunsdon, the Lord Chancellor, and the players were thereafter known as The Lord Chamberlain's Men.

3

Ascendant Fortune

During the years after university, Marlowe made friends with several other writers and with the free thinkers who congregated round Sir Walter Raleigh. Marlowe became particularly close to Thomas, the young cousin of Sir Francis Walsingham. Walsingham was interested in promising young men from Cambridge with the skills and aptitude for espionage and, as we have seen, the Privy Council thought sufficiently highly of Marlowe to intervene with the university authorities to demand that they award him his degree. Sir Francis also recognised Marlowe's theatrical talents. Professor Honan sees the popular theatre, with its touring companies, as an Elizabethan system of mass communication through which Walsingham could keep tabs on public opinion.

Thomas Walsingham was just three years Marlowe's senior and already working for his cousin at his London headquarters, known appropriately as 'Seething Lane', when Marlowe joined the service. Thomas's elder brother Edmund had died in 1589 so, in 1590, after the death of Sir Francis, Thomas inherited the family estate at Scadbury, near Chiselhurst in Kent. Scadbury became a sort of Camelot, a place that attracted poets and musicians as well as men of scientific enquiring minds, like the so-called 'circle of night' attached to Raleigh and the 'wizard earl' of Northumberland at Petworth, in Sussex. Scadbury had extensive grounds with gardens, fish ponds and a park of 400 acres. Here Marlowe was able to work in an extensive library and relax in the company of his closest friend, while at the same time being not far removed from his parental home in Canterbury.

Among Walsingham's coterie of friends was another poet, Thomas Watson, a suave and witty man of letters, much travelled and fluent in many languages. He and Marlowe became close friends and were living near to one another in 1589, in what is now Bishopsgate in London. It was there that they became involved in a dispute with a man called Bradley.

William Bradley owed £14 to an innkeeper by the name of Allen, the brother of Edward Alleyn, the actor. Bradley took exception to Watson because he had taken the part of his brother-in-law, Hugh Swift, a lawyer engaged by the innkeeper to help recover the debt. Bradley sent a fellow ruffian named Orrell to threaten Swift with dire consequences if he were to take Bradley to court. Not surprisingly this had the effect of making Swift seek legal protection from Orrell, obliging him to keep the peace.

At this point Bradley took out a counter summons against Swift, Allen and Watson. Marlowe was not then involved, but Bradley accosted him on the street near Watson's lodgings and a duel ensued. This attracted the attention of Watson and, as soon as Watson appeared on the scene, Bradley turned his attention to his main rival, crying 'Art thou now come, then I will have a bout with thee.' Marlowe apparently withdrew and took no further part in the fight, but Watson embraced Bradley's challenge, piercing Bradley through the heart, whereupon he died. The two friends, Watson and Marlowe, then waited for the arrival of the constable and were subseqently imprisoned in Newgate. Marlowe was there for 13 days, until released on a recognisance of £40. Watson remained in prison for five months, but was eventually released on the acceptance of his appeal on grounds of self-defence.

This 'Bradley affair' is often cited as evidence of Marlowe's volatility and tendency to get into trouble, but it is clear that he was a bystander, attacked by Bradley and in no way to blame for the affray. One is reminded of Romeo, drawn reluctantly into a street fight by Mercutio.

Another minor breach of the peace occurred in the spring of 1592 when the poet engaged in some kind of argument with a constable and beadle in Shoreditch. For this he was bound over to keep the peace in the sum of £20, in the following May. The parish officers, like Dogberry in *Much Ado About Nothing*, were probably too aware of their 'little brief authority', and Marlowe too proud to suffer insult without riposte.

Less easy to understand, or to excuse, is the incident in September 1592, when Marlowe was involved in a petty dispute with a tailor in Canterbury. According to the legal record, Marlowe attacked the tailor, William Corkine, with a stick and dagger. No one was seriously hurt, but Corkine claimed £5 in damages. Marlowe's father happened to be the constable at the time and paid 12d on his son's behalf as a surety. When the case came before the grand jury, it was thrown out as not worth consideration, thus sparing Marlowe the cost of his opponent's claim for damages. One wonders how many more times he would have found himself in trouble if it had not been for the affair at Deptford.

Potentially much more significant was the charge of being involved in false coinage. This occurred in January 1592, when he was in Flushing, Belgium, working for Lord Burghley. He may have been employed, at the time, trying to discover the source of illicit coinage, which was being used to pay the soldiers of the renegade English Catholic force, under

Sir William Stanley, at Nijmegen.

Marlowe had established contact with a Dutch goldsmith who demonstrated his skill by casting some coins in pewter. The resulting coins would not, of course, have had any value as they were clearly neither gold nor silver. At the time, Marlowe was sharing a room with Richard Baines, a distinctly shady character, who had been caught, while working as an undercover agent, at the seminary at Rheims, planning to poison the entire establishment. Marlowe makes use of this heinous plan in *The Jew of Malta*, where he has Barabas poison his daughter Abigail and the entire nunnery to which she has fled (III, iv, 97–107). Remarkably, Baines was released after a spell of imprisonment and was again engaged in some kind of espionage, when he learned of Marlowe's initiation into the arts of coining.

Baines reported the incident to Sir Robert Sidney, the Governor of Flushing, whereupon Marlowe made counter accusations against Baines, and the two were eventually taken before Lord Burleigh for questioning, on what could have been a very serious charge. The penalty for uttering false coinage could be death Burleigh evidently took Marlowe's side and there the matter ended, but it illustrates that there was no love lost between the two men.

There is a suggestion in Joseph Keaton's book, *Luvvies Labours Lost – A History of Forgotten Acting*, that Marlowe was working under the pseudonym of Tim Larkin – an anagram of Kit Marlin – during the summer of 1585. Keaton adds that much money was made by such actors working in the Low Countries.

Recent research by Peter Farey indicates that Marlowe was employed as a tutor to Arbella Stuart, the great, great granddaughter of Henry VII, in the years 1589 to 1592. Quite what this meant in hours of work, and how far he would have been resident in the various places Arabella occupied, is not entirely clear. Peter Farey shows, however, that Marlowe was partly living in the household of Bess of Hardwick, at Hardwick Old Hall, during the three and a half years to September 1592. This post probably came to Marlowe as a result of the machinations of Lord Burghley, who would have welcomed a trusted pair of ears within the household of the redoubtable duchess.

The connection with Burghley is testified by a letter sent to him by Bess complaining at the effrontery of Marlowe, who had had the temerity to ask for some reward for his labours. The quarrel, between Arbella's aunt and her tutor, is less important to us than the light it sheds on Burghley's interest in Marlowe. We have already noted the intervention by the Privy Council, in ensuring that Marlowe received his degree from Cambridge, but the fact that he worked as a tutor to the potential heir apparent, and that Burghley took a personal interest in his career, make it highly likely that whatever happened at Deptford was done with the knowledge and approval of the Queen's first minister, if not of the Queen herself.

4

Death at Deptford

Life continued to bring Marlowe fame and some degree of fortune from his popularity as a poet and playwright. After the rapturous reception of both *Tamburlaine* plays, he had further acclaim for his *Dr Faustus* and the portrayal of recent history in *The Massacre at Paris*. At the same time, he was working on the historical antecedent to his trilogy of *Henry VI* and composing the elegiac poems on *Hero and Leander* and *Venus and Adonis*. Enough, one would have thought, to keep anyone out of trouble. He had the library at Scadbury in which to work and probably made use of the great storehouse of knowledge accumulated by the Earl of Northumberland at Petworth.

He was at the peak of his popularity and recognised as the greatest poet of the day, 'the muse's darling', when suddenly the world crashed round him. He was labelled an atheist and accused of all manner of antisocial activity. Told to report daily to the Privy Council, he lived in fear of torture or even of being sent to the gallows.

The crisis had its origin in the puritanical zeal of Archbishop Whitgift, who had become the most influential figure in the Privy Council. Whitgift had obtained a decree forbidding the publication of any book or pamphlet unless previously authorised by himself or the Bishop of London. He thus had power over printing and over the punishment of anyone printing seditious or slanderous books. In February 1593, the Privy Council was given power to punish any person challenging the authority of the Church.

Then, on 3 May a letter, threatening the Huguenot community, was posted on their church wall. It was full of references to Marlowe's plays and was evidently an attempt to incriminate him. On 11 May, a bill was passed allowing the Privy Council to 'Search in any of the chambers, studies, chests or other like places, for all manner of writing and papers that might give you light for the discovery of the libellers … you shall by authority hereof put them to the torture in Bridewell, and by the extremity thereof draw them to discover their knowledge' (Charles Nicholl, *The Reckoning: The Murder of Christopher Marlowe*, 1992).

The following day the rooms of Thomas Kyd were ransacked by the authorities and an atheistic tract was found among his papers. Kyd later claimed that it belonged to Marlowe, for whom the Privy Council lost no time in issuing a warrant of arrest. What might have happened if Marlowe had followed Kyd onto the rack? Who else might then be incriminated? For Raleigh and the 'School of Night', the storm clouds were gathering and Marlowe was at the centre of the threat posed to free thinkers throughout the kingdom. Something had to be done.

Marlowe was living at Scadbury when the summons was served. He was not immediately thrown into jail, like Kyd, but was given 14 days' bail, during which time he had to report daily to the Privy Council at Nonsuch, the royal castle near Cheam in Surrey, so called on account of its exceptional beauty, where the Queen happened to be staying at the time. If his friends were to evade the very real chance of being caught in a puritanical witch-hunt, they had to do something to remove Marlowe from the scene. The easiest way would have been to murder him, but apart from human sympathy and personal affection for Marlowe, such a course might well have added suspicions that his death was too convenient for his fellow free-thinkers. The purge would not stop with Marlowe. He had to be silenced in some other way.

If Marlowe were to escape abroad or go into hiding, there would still be a hunt for his accomplices and sympathisers. He might even be followed to some other country and hounded or punished, as Tyndale had been for publishing the first translation of the Bible into English. Somehow it had to appear that Marlowe had died without any blame attaching to his supposed killer. Once out of the way, he would require another identity and some means of contacting his friends in England. What is more, if he were to produce further works of literature, they could not be launched onto the world stage under his own name.

Some obliging front-man had to be found, while Marlowe himself must appear to have died, and to have done so through his own recklessness, in order that no one else would be charged with his murder.

Quite how and when the plot to fake his death was hatched, we cannot say, but it is likely that Marlowe himself was put on board a boat leaving Deptford before noon and that his friends were left to concoct a credible explanation for his disappearance. By the evening, a body was found that could be passed off as that of Marlowe, while his friends were exonerated by a story that put the blame squarely on the impetuous and uncivil behaviour of the poet himself.

In Deptford, he met with three friends at the house of a woman called Eleanor Bull, who was distantly related to Lord Burghley, and after a day of apparently friendly discourse, Marlowe was said to have been stabbed in self-defence by one of his companions. The matter seemed beyond doubt.

Marlowe's body was identified by his friends and the facts verified by the coroner. His body was later buried in the churchyard at Deptford. So the case rested until 1925, when Dr Leslie Hotson discovered the actual coroner's report, and questions began to be asked.

The coroner's account states that Marlowe met with three friends, Robert Poley, Nicholas Skeres and Ingram Frizer. Poley was the country's foremost spy working for Thomas Walsingham. He had been approached by Babbington to assist in his plot to overthrow Queen Elizabeth, but, instead, he betrayed him to Sir Francis Walsingham. Nicholas Skeres had also been involved in Babbington's downfall and was occasionally employed by Walsingham. The third man, Frizer, was also a long-standing retainer of Walsingham, who had engaged in some shady business dealings with Skeres.

After a day conversing together, a quarrel is said to have broken out between the three men over the payment of a paltry bill. In the otherwise official Latin account, this is referred to as '*le recknynge*'. Marlowe was said to be seated or lying behind Frizer, when he took out his knife and attempted to strike Frizer on his head. In the ensuing struggle, Marlowe was stabbed with his own weapon and died, 'the coward conquest of a wretch's knife' as Sonnet 74 says. Frizer thus escaped blame, having acted in self-defence.

Everything was done to make it seem that Marlowe was entirely and solely to blame for his own death. It would have been grossly unfair on Ingram Frizer if he had been punished for Marlowe's murder. An inquest was held the next day, at Deptford, at which the jury accepted the story told by the three witnesses. The coroner, William Danby, was the Queen's own, rather than the normal coroner appointed for the area, because Deptford fell 'within the verge' of her royal authority while she was in residence at Nonsuch. It is not inconceivable therefore that Danby was leaned upon to accept the official version of what happened at Deptford.

But the story just doesn't ring true. Why would two friends squabble over a trifling sum after spending the day in conversation? Is it likely that any man would stab another on his head from behind in a petty argument over paying a bill? And what of the other two friends? Did they simply let it all happen and not intervene in any way? Modern medical opinion questions whether an injury, of the sort described, would have been fatal, at least, not immediately. It also seems curious that the man who 'killed' Marlowe, Ingram Frizer, was given a mere four weeks in jail and then returned to service with the poet's friend and employer, Thomas Walsingham.

David More has identified the presence, in a nearby prison, of one John Penry, who was awaiting execution as a heretic. Assuming that Walsingham and the Queen's chief ministers colluded in the subterfuge, Penry's body could have been mutilated and passed off as that of Marlowe.

A similar fate awaited Barnardine in the play *Measure for Measure*. When Claudio is condemned to death, the Duke, disguised as a holy man, hatches a plot to substitute for Claudio's body that of a condemned criminal, Barnardine: 'Let this Barnardine be this morning executed, and his head borne to Angelo,' says the Duke. The Provost objects that, 'Angelo hath seen them both and will discover the favour.' To which the Duke replies, 'O death's a great disguiser; and you may add to it. Shave his head and tie the beard; and say it was the desire of the penitent to be so bar'd before his death. You know the course is common' (*Measure for Measure*, Act 4, sc. 2, 171–78).

While Marlowe was on bail, the case against him was made

far more damning by the revelations of Richard Baines, the same man who had reported him for false coinage in Flushing. Hearing of Marlowe's arrest, Baines set about gathering as much information as possible with which to tarnish his reputation further. He presented his findings to the Privy Council in what has become known as 'the Baines note'.

Mrs Wraight reproduces a copy of the Baines note in her book on the sonnets (226) from the document in the British Library. It is reprinted here, with permission:

> A note Containing the opinion of on[e] Christopher Marly Concerning his Damnable Judgment of Religion, and scorn of gods word.
>
> That the Indians and many Authors of antiquity have assuredly writen aboue 16 thousand yeares agone wher as Adam is proued to haue lived w'hin 6 thousand yeares.
> He affirmeth that Moyses was but a Juqler, & that one Heriots being Sir W Raleighs man can do more then he.
> That Moyses made the Jewes to travell 11 yeares in the wildernes, (wch Jorney might haue bin Done in lesse then one yeare) ere they Came to the promised land to thintent that those who were privy to most of his subtilties might perish and so an everlasting superstition Remain in the hartes of the people.
> That the first beginning of Religioun was only to keep men in awe
> That it was an easy matter for Moyses being brought up in all the artes of the Egiptians to abuse the Jewes being a rude & grosse people.

That Christ was a bastard and his mother dishonest.

That he was the sonne of a Carpenter, and that if the Jewes among whome he was borne did Crucify him theie best knew him and whence he Came.

That Christ deserved better to Dy then Barrabas and that the Jewes made a good Choise, though Barrabas were both a thief and murtherer.

That if there be any god or any good Religion, then it is in the papistes because the service of god is performed wth more Cerimonies, as Elevation of the mass, organs, singing men, Shaven Crownes & cta, that all protestantes are Hypocriticall asses.

That if he were put to write a new Religion, he would undertake both a more Exellent and Admirable methode and that all the new testament is filthily written.

That the woman of Samaria & her sister were whores & that Christ knew them dishonestly,

That St John the Evangelist was bedfellow to C[hrist] and leaned alwaies in his bosome, that he used him as the sinners of Sodoma.

That all they that loue not Tobacco & Boies were fooles.

That all the apostles were fishermen and base fellowes neyther of wit nor worth, that Paull only had wit but he was a timerous fellow in bidding men to be subiect to magistrates against his Conscience.

That he had as good Right to Coine as the Queene of England, and that he was acquainted wth one poole a prisoner in newgate who hath great Skill in mixture of mettals and having learned some thinges of him he ment through help of a Cunninge stamp maker to Coin ffrench Crownes pistolets and English shillinges.

That if Christ would have instituted the sacrament wth more Ceremoniall Reverence it would have bin had in more admiration, that it would have bin much better being administred in a Tobacco pipe.

That the Angell Gabriell was Baud to the holy ghost, because he brought the salutation to Mary.

That on[e] Ric Cholmley hath Confessed that he was perswaded by Marloe's Reasons to become an Atheist.

These thinges, wth many other shall by good & honest witnes be aproved to be his opinions and Comon Speeches, and that this Marlow doth not only hould them himself, but almost into every Company he Cometh he perswades men to Atheism willing them not to be afeard of bugbeares and hobgoblins, and utterly scorning both god and his ministers as J Richard Baines will Justify & approue both by mine oth and the testimony of many honest men, and almost al men with whome he hath Conversed any time will testify the same, and as J think all men in Cristianity ouqht to indevor that the mouth of so dangerous a member may be stopped, he saith likewise that he hath quoted a number of Contrarieties oute of the Scripture wch he hath giuen to some great men who in Convenient time shalbe named. When these thinges shalbe Called in question the witnes shalbe produced.

RICHARD BAMES [Baines]

Much of this is at the level of schoolboy humour, and none of it originated in Marlowe, in so far as every one of the allegations had been previously published. But when assembled together in this form at this time, it was serious enough to ruin Marlowe's reputation overnight. His chances of a successful career were irreparably ruined. After Deptford, he was not only dead but damned.

The views expressed in the Baines note are the sort of thing a young man might well have voiced in the company of his friends, though why he would have written them down is unclear. Others had faced torture and death for similar beliefs. A month earlier, John Greenwood had been hanged for writing subversive tracts. Lord Burghley had tried to save him, but the power of Archbishop Whitgift was at its height and heretics fell victim to his puritanical witch-hunt. The words ascribed to Marlowe were enough to have put him in prison and tortured, and, if he had succumbed to torture, who else would have felt the finger pointing to them as equally heretical? 'The late 16th century', says Mrs Wraight, 'was marked by terrible exhibitions of religious intolerance with the active suppression of free thought and scientific questioning' (*The Story the Sonnets Tell*, 270).

Archbishop Whitgift would have relished the chance to silence one so close to Raleigh. Marlowe's death at Deptford happened in the nick of time. He had been given 14 days bail on condition that he reported daily to the Privy Council. On the tenth day of his bail he met with his 'accident'. Dead men tell no tales, and his friends and acquaintances could breathe more freely.

5

The Story the Sonnets Tell

While his friends concocted the details of his demise, Marlowe himself had to make his escape, probably to France. Deptford had been chosen for its proximity to the Thames and the Channel crossing. He was well used to the sea voyage, having made several journeys to France and the Low Countries as an agent of Walsingham. He was also familiar with the necessity of keeping a low profile and probably already had a convenient alias.

Mrs Wraight has argued that Marlowe was a Freemason and that this provided a convenient cover for his operations after Deptford. 'It was Bacon's society, the Freemasons, who acted to protect the stricken poet, by providing a cover of anonymity – total anonymity – behind which he was concealed' (*The Story the Sonnets Tell*, page 288).

Marlowe was probably ignorant of the defamation of character that was heaped on him, following his escape from England, but it was necessary for the protection of his friends. The more his character was trashed, the less sympathy would his death arouse, and it would be said, with confidence, that 'he had it coming', he deserved to die. The notion of poetic justice and of wickedness incurring punishment was widely accepted. Thus Marlowe's character was tarnished beyond redemption; he was an atheist, a blasphemer, a homosexual and his death was thoroughly deserved. The sonnets suggest that he was utterly mortified when he learned the extent of his own disgrace. Not only was he now an outlaw, unable to see his family and friends again, but he was a man whose reputation was utterly ruined. Daryl Pinksen in his book, *Marlowe's Ghost*, reprints several passages from contemporary writers to illustrate the 'vile esteem' into which Marlowe fell, as a result of the calumnies heaped on him after the affair at Deptford. Two such passages are given here. Thomas Beard in his *Theater of God's Judgments* (1597), wrote:

> Nor inferior to any of the former in Atheism and impiety, and equal to all in manner of punishment was one of our own nation, of fresh and late memory, called Marlin, by profession a scholar brought up from his youth in the University of Cambridge, but by practice a playmaker, and a poet of Scurrility, who by giving too large a swing to his own wit, and suffering his lust to have the full reigns, fell (not without just desert) to that outrage and extremity, that he denied God and his son Christ, and not only in word blasphemed the trinity, but also (as it is credibly reported) wrote books against it, affirming our saviour to be but a deceiver, and Moses to be but a conjurer and seducer of the people, and the holy Bible to be but vain and idle stories, and all religion but a device of policy. But see what a hook the Lord put in the nostrils of this barking dog: It so fell out, that in London streets as he purposed to stab one whom he sought a grudge unto with his dagger, the other party perceiving so

avoided the stroke, that withal catching hold of his wrist, he stabbed his own dagger into his own head, in such sort, that notwithstanding all the means of surgery that could be wrought, he shortly died thereof.

The second passage, reprinted here from Pinksen (50–51), is taken from another rabidly religious work, *The Thunderbolt of God's Wrath Against Hard Hearted and Stiff-necked Sinners*, by Edmund Rudierde (1618):

We read of one Marlin, a Cambridge scholar, who was a poet, and a filthy Play-maker, this wretch accounted that meek servant of God Moses to be but a Conjurer, and our sweet Saviour to be but a seducer and deceiver of the people. But harken ye brainsick and Profane poets, and Players, that bewitch idle ears with foolish vanities: what fell upon this profane wretch, having a quarrel against one whom he met in a street in London, and would have stabbed him: But the party perceiving his villainy prevented him with catching his hand, and running his own dagger into his brains, and so blaspheming and cursing, he yielded up his stinking breath: mark this ye Players, that live by making fools laugh at sin and wickedness.

These are clearly the extreme sort of puritanical views that would lead to the closure of the theatres during the government of Cromwell. Protestant England would not have offered a safe homecoming to Kit Marlowe.

In 1993, Dolly Wraight published her book entitled *The*

Story the Sonnets Tell. She had written a biography of Marlowe some years previously, but had been increasingly convinced that the official verdict on his death was not reliable. Her doubts were strengthened as a result of reading the coroner's report discovered in 1925 by Dr Hotson. Mrs Wraight was convinced that many of the sonnets were autobiographical, telling of Marlowe's life after a faked death at Deptford.

Read in this light, the sonnets unlock the story of Marlowe's flight from England and his painful realisation that he would never be able to enjoy the celebrity and personal happiness he had known among his friends and family. The sonnets relate to a number of aspects of the poet's life, but about a dozen can be seen as lamenting his fate as he leaves his country and comrades, with no hope of ever returning.

Sonnets 26 and 27 evoke the physical and mental exhaustion Marlowe experienced after his flight from his friends, and from his patron Walsingham in particular.

26

Lord of my love, to whom in vassalage
Thy merit hath my duty strongly knit,
To thee I send this written embassage
To witness duty, not to show my wit;
Duty so great which wit so poor as mine
May make seem bare in wanting words to show it,
But that I hope some good conceit of thine
In thy soul's thought, all naked, will bestow it,
Till whatsoever star that guides my moving
Points on me graciously with fair aspect,
And puts apparel on my tattered loving
To show me worthy of thy sweet respect.
　　Then may I dare to boast how I do love thee;

Till then, not show my head where thou mayst prove
me.

Likewise, Sonnet 27 evokes the sense of a travel-weary poet,
wrestling with feelings of dejection and despair, but restored to
courage and fortitude by remembrance of his absent friend:

27

Weary with toil I haste me to my bed,
The dear repose for limbs with travel tired;
But then begins a journey in my head
To work my mind where body's work's expired;
For then my thoughts, far from where I abide,
Intend a zealous pilgrimage to thee,
And keep my drooping eyelids open wide,
Looking on darkness which the blind do see:
Save that my soul's imaginary sight
Presents thy shadow to my sightless view,
Which like a jewel hung in ghastly night
Makes black night beauteous and her old face new.
    Lo, thus by day my limbs, by night my mind,
    For thee, and for myself, no quiet find.

There follows another poignant lament for the loss of his
friends. But once again, the poem ends with the reflection that
the memory of Walsingham's company is enough to restore
his spirits:

29

When, in disgrace with fortune and men's eyes,
I all alone beweep my outcast state,

And trouble deaf heaven with my bootless cries,
And look upon myself and curse my fate,
Wishing me like to one more rich in hope,
Featured like him, like him with friends possessed,
Desiring this man's art and that man's scope,
With what I most enjoy contented least:
Yet in these thoughts myself almost despising,
Haply I think on thee, and then my state,
Like to the lark at break of day arising
From sullen earth, sings hymns at heaven's gate;
    For thy sweet love remembered such wealth brings
    That then I scorn to change my state with kings.

And a similar sentiment is expressed in the following sonnet:

30

When to the sessions of sweet silent thought
I summon up remembrance of things past,
I sigh the lack of many a thing I sought,
And with old woes new wail my dear time's waste.
Then can I drown an eye unused to flow
For precious friends hid in death's dateless night,
And weep afresh love's long-since-cancelled woe,
And moan th'expense of many a vanished sight.
Then can I grieve at grievances forgone,
And heavily from woe to woe tell o'er
The sad account of fore-bemoaned moan,
Which I new pay as if not paid before.
    But if the while I think on thee, dear friend,
    All losses are restored, and sorrows end.

Sonnet 31 is also in the same vein – Walsingham has become

for him a sort of amalgam of all the love he misses from his lost circle of friends:

31

Thy bosom is endeared with all hearts,
Which I by lacking have supposed dead,
And there reigns love, and all love's loving parts,
And all those friends which I thought buried.
How many a holy and obsequious tear
Hath dear religious love stol'n from mine eye
As interest of the dead, which now appear
But things removed that hidden in thee lie!
Thou art the grave where buried love doth live,
Hung with the trophies of my lovers gone,
Who all their parts of me did give:
That due of many now is thine alone.
    Their images I loved I view in thee
    And thou, all they, hast all the all of me.

Some of the sonnets describe his journey across France and the Alps to Italy, while at the same time lamenting the dark event at Deptford, when his rising fame and fortune were suddenly eclipsed. Sonnet 33 is a beautiful evocation of mountains and morning sunshine, clothed in a mist. Marlowe compares the cloud-covered sun to the sun of Walsingham's favour, of which the Deptford episode deprived him after a brief hour:

33

Full many a glorious morning have I seen
Flatter the mountain tops with sovereign eye,
Kissing with golden face the meadows green,

Gilding pale streams with heavenly alchemy;
Anon permit the basest clouds to ride
With ugly rack on his celestial face,
And from the forlorn world his visage hide,
Stealing unseen to west with this disgrace.
Even so my sun one early morn did shine
With all triumphant splendour on my brow;
But out, alack, he was but one hour mine;
The region cloud hath masked him from me now.
    Yet him for this my love no whit disdaineth:
        Suns of the world may stain when heaven's sun
staineth.

Once again, in Sonnet 34, Marlowe laments the loss of his reputation. He appears to blame Walsingham for encouraging him to depart, without fully appreciating the shame that was to be heaped upon him in consequence. Walsingham evidently apologised for the attacks on his honour. Marlowe initially objects that such apologies do nothing to erase his sense of shame, but finally admits that the tears of his friend outweigh all his suffering.

34

Why didst thou promise such a beauteous day
And make me travel forth without my cloak,
To let base clouds o'r take me in my way,
Hiding thy brav'ry in their rotten smoke?
'Tis not enough that through the cloud thou break
To dry the rain on my storm-beaten face,
For no man well of such a salve can speak
That heals the wound and cures not the disgrace.
Nor can thy shame give physic to my grief;

Though thou repent, yet I have still the loss.
Th' offender's sorrow lends but weak relief
To him that bears the strong offence's cross.
    Ah, but those tears are pearl which thy love sheds,
    And they are rich, and ransom all ill deeds.

Mrs Wraight identifies many more of the sonnets as autobiographical, and indicative of Marlowe's deep affection and sense of indebtedness to Walsingham. Perhaps the most graphic is number 50 which mentions the 'beast that bears' him on which he depended for part of his travels and which bore him ever further away from his friends in England:

50

How heavy do I journey on my way,
When what I seek – my weary travel's end –
Doth teach that ease and that repose to say
'Thus far the miles are measured from thy friend.'
The beast that bears me, tired with my woe,
Plods dully on to bear that weight in me,
As if by some instinct the wretch did know
His rider loved not speed, being made from thee.
The bloody spur cannot provoke him on
That sometimes anger thrusts into his hide,
Which heavily he answers with a groan
More sharp to me than spurring to his side;
    For that same groan doth put this in my mind:
    My grief lies onward and my joy behind.

Let us leave the story the sonnets tell with two of the best known of all. Every reader will know Sonnet 71 as a plea to his friends not to grieve for him in death, since he would not

have them saddened by his parting. But if it is addressed to
Walsingham in particular, it urges him not to let others know
that he is grieving for Marlowe, lest some of Marlowe's shame
attaches to Walsingham and possibly leads to exposure of the
whole plot to keep him safely out of reach.

71

No longer mourn for me when I am dead
Than you shall hear the surly sullen bell
Give warning to the world that I am fled
From this vile world with vilest worms to dwell.
Nay, if you read this line, remember not
The hand that writ it; for I love you so.
That I in your sweet thoughts would be forgot
If thinking on me then should make you woe.
Or, if, I say, you look upon this verse
When I perhaps compounded am with clay,
Do not so much as my poor name rehearse,
But let your love even with my life decay,
　　Lest the wise world should look into your moan
　　And mock you with me after I am gone.

Sonnet 81 takes this theme further, and imagines future
ages 'when all the breathers of this world are dead'. Having
forgotten Marlowe, the world will still remember Walsingham
through the poems addressed to him.

81

Or shall I live your epitaph to make,
Or you survive when I in earth am rotten.
From hence your memory death cannot take,

Although in me each part will be forgotten.
Your name from hence immortal life shall have,
Though I, once gone, to all the world must die.
The earth can yield me but a common grave
When you entombed in men's eues shall lie.
Your monument shall be my gentle verse,
Which eyes not yet created shall o'er read,
And tongues to be your being shall rehearse
When all the breathers of this world are dead.
   You still shall live – such virtue hath my pen –
     Where breath most breathes, even in the mouths
     of men.

There is much more to the sonnets than lamentation for the poet's exile, but the sonnets reproduced here testify to his grief at the sudden loss of his good name and to the pain of separation from his patron, Walsingham, and from his many other friends. They are clearly autobiographical.

6

At the Court of Navarre

If the predominant mood of the sonnets of exile is one of
self-pity and dismay at his banishment, that of the plays set
in Italy and Navarre is one of fun and exuberance. This must
have been a period of unexpected *joie de vivre*, a release from the
strains of life in England, from fear of persecution and bigotry,
from living under the cloudy skies of Kent to revelling in the
warmth of the Mediterranean sun. One suspects that after the
initial anguish and despair at leaving England had subsided,
Marlowe grew to appreciate the change in his circumstances.
He was free from political suspicion and fear of religious
fanaticism. He was living in a warm climate, free to explore
beautiful cities and indulge in good food and wine – and, no
doubt, the company of beautiful women. Life surely offered
some consolation for the poet in exile.

How Marlowe made his living we don't know, but he would
have been provided with sufficient money to survive until he
found employment. He may well have been given some kind
of introduction to the court of Henry of Navarre, for it is
difficult to imagine how anyone unfamiliar with the artificial
ambience of the court of Navarre, in *Love's Labour's Lost*, could
have penned so delightful and intimate a picture of aristocrats
at play.

This is taken to be one of Shakespeare's first plays, and

indeed it is likely to have been the first penned in exile, based on personal observation of courtly manners in the retinue of Henry of Navarre. The French scholar, Abel Lefranc, argues that *Love's Labour's Lost* could only have been written by one conversant with his court.

If Marlowe did obtain some kind of position in the household of Navarre, or some other great nobleman, there would have been diplomatic contacts enabling him to communicate with his friends in England. He may have made use of erstwhile colleagues, in Walsingham's secret service, to forward his dramatic scripts to Richard Field, the printer at St Paul's churchyard. Once in England, Marlowe's works had to be published under someone else's name.

Someone had to be found to act as 'midwife'. An impecunious actor might be just the sort of person required. The man who evidently agreed to do this was William Shakespeare, or more properly, Shaksper, of Stratford upon Avon. He was familiar with the world of actors and playwrights and he was known to Richard Field as coming from his home town.

The first piece to appear under Shakespeare's name was the poem *Venus and Adonis*. Marlowe had translated the poems of Ovid while at university and he was steeped in the literature of classical antiquity. This poem was clearly written while still in England, but it could no longer be ascribed to Marlowe.

It was the first time Shakespeare's name ever appeared in print and it was a very odd piece for him to have chosen if it really did proceed from the pen of a jobbing actor who lacked any formal education, almost as odd as the choice of courtly frippery in *Love's Labour's Lost*.

William Shakespeare was in fact a sensible choice. He was exactly the same age as Marlowe and he was familiar with the world of acting and the theatre. Above all, he was probably impecunious and willing to make a quick buck if the opportunity arose, so he readily agreed to be the front-man for anything Field put his name to. In fact, he didn't limit his generosity to Marlowe, but also fronted the works of several other playwrights. How he was rewarded is not known, but it is suggested that in return he received shares in the acting company to which he belonged.

Everything we know about William Shaksper of Stratford indicates that he was an astute businessman, quick to prosecute those who crossed him in matters of business. Generations of Stratfordian scholars have tried in vain to find evidence of his literary prowess. He left no letters, and his will contained no reference to books or papers. He left no samples of his handwriting except for some signatures, none of which resembled the others. The townsfolk of Stratford never thought they had a genius in their midst until about 150 years after his death, when the actor, David Garrick, began the great glorification of Shakespeare that has made his birthplace the most popular place of pilgrimage in England.

Thus, while Kit Marlowe suffered an irrevocable eclipse, the name of William Shakespeare was destined to become that of the greatest man in English history. Whenever it is argued that Shakespeare had not the skill nor the life experience to have written the works ascribed to him, his devotees reply that he was a natural genius and, moreover, there is the panegyric of Ben Jonson to attest the truth of his authorship. Jonson did indeed speak of the 'Swan of Avon' and 'divine Shakespeare', but there is doubt as to whether he was speaking from the heart.

Jonson was well known for his ability to bend the truth and the flattering references he makes to Shakespeare in the preface to the First Folio can be seen as mere hype, intended to make the work sell. It would not have been in his own interests to reveal the truth, even at that stage, for too many people would have been liable to prosecution for their part in the deception. As the passage quoted above from Edmund Rudierde, in 1618, demonstrates, the mud heaped on Marlowe had stuck fast.

If we want to know what Jonson really thought of Shakespeare, we need look no further than his play *Every Man out of His Humour*. Daryl Pinksen, in his book, *Marlowe's Ghost*, suggests that the character, Macilente, in Jonson's play, is a portrayal of Marlowe. Macilente enters at the start of the play wandering the countryside, reading a book. He compares his own poor state with that of more fortunate men who are respected for their money, power and learning, while he, Macilente, or Marlowe, bemoans his fate:

> when I view myself,
> Having before observed this man is great,
> Mighty and feared; that loved and highly favoured:
> A third thought wise and learned; a fourth rich,
> And therefore honoured; a fifth rarely featured;
> A sixth admired for his nuptial fortunes
> When I see these, I say, and view myself,
> I wish the organs of my sight were cracked.

Macilente conceals himself behind a hedge, and hears Sogliardo boasting of his good fortune. Pinksen suggests that this character, Sogliardo, is in fact Shakespeare. Macilente fumes to himself at the bragging of this upstart: 'Why should such a prick-eared hind as this be rich?' There then follows a passage in which Sogliardo talks of his desire for a coat of arms, an ambition he shares with Shakespeare's father. Another character in the play, Carlo Buffone, asks if Sogliardo has his coat of arms, to which he replies: 'I'faith, I thank them; I can write myself gentleman now; here's my patent, it cost me thirty pound, by this breath.'

When asked what the arms look like, he says, 'Marry, sir, it is your boar without a head, rampant,' to which Buffone replies, 'I commend the herald's wit, he has deciphered him well: a swine without a head, without brain, wit, anything indeed, ramping to gentility.' When Sogliardo proceeds to boast about the wording on his crest, another character, Puntarvolo, comments, in an aside: 'It is the most vile, foolish, observed, palpable, and ridiculous escutcheon that ever this eye survised.' When Sogliardo asks what he thinks of the wording, Puntarvolo replies: 'Let the word be, "Not without mustard": your crest is very rare, sir.'

Sogliardo's crest is evidently a parody of that chosen by the Shakespeares: 'Not Without Right'. Such an outright lampooning by Jonson of his 'friend' Shakespeare is hard to equate with the well-known plaudits of the First Folio. Indeed, the explanation must be that Jonson had no genuine admiration for the man. The picture he leaves us, in his own play, is that of a bucolic ignoramus, an oaf of Avon, rather than a swan. Later in the play, Sogliardo talks of building his own tomb, as Shakespeare did at Stratford. The wisdom of such a move lying in the thought that: 'your heirs may hap forget it else'.

If we look at the character of Macilente, as described by another character in the play, we may perhaps glimpse some of the qualities Jonson saw in Christopher Marlowe. Macilente is described caustically as: 'a lean mongrel, he looks as if he were chop-fallen with barking at other men's good fortunes: 'ware how you offend him; he carries oil and fire in his pen, will scald where it drops; his spirit is like powder, quick, violent; he will blow a man up with a jest. I fear him worse than a rotten wall does the cannon; shake an hour after its first report.

Away come not near him.' It has often struck me as curious that we have no account of Shakespeare's acerbic wit, 'oil and fire … scalding where it drops', causing offence or resulting in actions for defamation. As a front-man and mere *nom de plume*, Shakespeare clearly ran no such risk.

7

Italian Odyssey

Some time after leaving the court of Henry of Navarre, Marlowe evidently made his way to Italy and probably to Padua or Verona, the city in which more of his plays are set than any other. He was still a young man and we can picture him entering into the kind of lifestyle and activities that would engage the interests of a lively young adventurer. Like his French play, *Love's Labour's Lost*, his first plays set in Italy are predominantly about the vicissitudes of love. *The Two Gentlemen of Verona* should, perhaps, more truly be called 'one gentleman', Valentine, for his friend, Proteus, behaves throughout in such an appalling way that one cannot, by any stretch of the imagination, call him a gentleman. He traduces his own first love, betrays his best friend and attempts to seduce his friend's sweetheart.

Both young men are about to do what every aspiring noble youth was expected to do: to present themselves at the court of a local lord, in this case the Emperor Charles V, who had been briefly in Milan to receive homage from the local duke in 1533 (Roe 69–71). Antonio, the father of Proteus, is urged to send his son to the royal court:

> There shall he practise tilts and tournaments,
> Hear sweet discourse, converse with noblemen,

And be in the eye of every exercise
Worthy of his youth and nobleness of birth.

Act I, sc. ii, lines 31–34

In fact, the Emperor did not stay long in Italy and the two young men were able to seek other amusement. Valentine sings his famous song to Sylvia and is pressed into service as the leader of a band of outlaws, rather like Robin Hood. The lovers converge on a wood to the east of the city and all is resolved; Proteus even gains forgiveness from the generous Julia.

The play is often ridiculed as farcical and it is quoted as proof of the writer's ignorance of Italian topography. Richard Paul Roe, however, an American lawyer who made it his life's work to research Shakespeare's references to Italy, has shown how wide of the mark these critics can be.

Valentine is about to take ship for Milan, in the opening scene, and conventional criticism has charged the writer with ignorance of basic geography because Verona and Milan were land-locked, inland cities. In fact, however, they were linked by a canal. Verona was at the centre of an important trade route through the Brenner Pass in the Alps and via the River Adige to the Mediterranean. At the end of the fourteenth century, a new canal, the 'Naviglio Martesana', was dug 29 kilometres eastward of Milan to link with the river Adda. There was, in fact, a canal surrounding Milan, abutting its ancient walls, and a newer canal, deeper and wider, was built in 1573 to enable cargo ships to enter directly into the city.

Roe also found evidence, on a map of 1713, that there was a canal route linking the Rivers Po and Adige. Marlowe, probably living in Verona at the time, would have been well aware of these communications by water, enabling Valentine and Proteus to make their way to Milan by boat. The lovesick

Julia, by contrast, is determined to make her way by land, disguised as a boy to reduce some of the hazards of such a journey for an unaccompanied female.

If Marlowe's first plays written in exile were centred on the behaviour of young noblemen at court, the next was almost entirely concerned with young love in the tragic story of *Romeo and Juliet*. Once again, critics have averred that the writer betrays ignorance of local topography. For instance, in the opening scene of the play, Romeo's mother asks one of his friends if he has seen anything of her son. He answers that he saw him early that morning 'in a grove of sycamore trees'. Commentators had always assumed this to be a simple mistake by the playwright, since sycamores were a common sight in his native England but hardly likely to occur in Verona. Roe proved they were wrong, and, in his book, *The Shakespeare Guide to Italy*, he has a photograph showing sycamores growing today outside the western walls of the city. The illustrations shown in the plate section are of the Porta Palio outside the walls, as well as a shot from inside the gate, showing sycamores growing much as they did in the late Middle Ages.

Roe established that the story, sometimes said to be original to Shakespeare, was in fact an old Italian tale, recorded by a nobleman of Vicenza in 1535. Neither he nor subsequent borrowers of the story mentioned sycamores, yet there they are to this day. What peculiar flight of fancy could have led someone sitting in London or Stratford to record such a detail? Marlowe was evidently using his own knowledge of Verona.

The play begins with a street fight looming between the two houses of Montague and Capulet. It is abruptly halted by the arrival of Prince Escalus. He orders Capulet to accompany him on his way, but tells old Montague to appear before him at 'Freetown, our common judgement place'. In other words, Capulet is let off with a private rebuke, while Montague is to be arraigned at a common court of law to hear his punishment. Roe decided to track down the location of Escalus's place of 'common judgement'. He found it about ten miles south-west of Verona, at Villafranca Di Nuova. The remains of this place, where feudal law was promulgated, still stand as an imposing reminder of the dominance of Escalus, or della Scala, in the medieval world.

Roe delved into the background to the story and found that the great Prince Escalus did not rule for long, having succeeded his father in 1301 and died in 1304. Local opinion never doubts that the story belongs to 1302. The della Scala family are commonly known as the Scaligero and they had many castles in the surrounding countryside, but there was only one place from which they would make public pronouncements: the castle tower of Villafranca outside Verona. Roe points out that in singling out Montague for public censure, Escalus was demonstrating an unfair bias against him and his house. The same bias is detected in the Prince's decision to banish Romeo, a Montague, while the Capulets receive more lenient treatment. This departure of the Prince from his proper impartiality would have been seen by the citizens of Verona as boding ill for the ensuing drama.

Tourists gravitate in their thousands to view the places mentioned in Shakespeare's story. In response to their wishes, the Veronese have obliged by erecting a balcony from which Juliet might have delivered her pathetic plea: 'Wherefore art thou Romeo?' No such balcony existed until 1934 and it would have been somewhat remiss of her father to have left her alone in a bedroom with a balcony facing the street – almost an invitation to some hot-blooded youth. There is in fact no mention of a balcony in the play, only a 'window'.

Other places mentioned in the text can still be seen. The houses of the two families and the little church of St Peter, the one mentioned three times, in Act III, Scene v, where Juliet's father insists she must be married to the County Paris. The St Francis monastery where Friar Laurence had his cell, in which the lovers were bound in matrimony, is still there, as is the family crypt of the Capulets, where Juliet's body lay and the final scenes of the tragedy unfold: 'For never was there story of such woe as this of Juliet and her Romeo.'

While tourists flock in their thousands to worship at the shrine of Juliet, no such magnetism draws them to the house of Romeo. Even the stone information board is defaced almost beyond legibility. Friar Lawrence's Monastery is venerated as the scene both of the marriage and of Juliet's tragic suicide. There is even an ethereal modern sculpture by a Chinese artist testifying to the universal appeal of the fate of the young lovers.

Another early play set in northern Italy is *The Taming of the Shrew*. It, too, has characters using the canals of the time to make journeys of some distance. Here again scholars have assumed Shakespeare's ignorance when Lucentio announces that he has 'arrived for fruitful Lombardy' from Pisa. Roe suggests the preposition 'from' should be substituted in place of 'for' and then shows how Lucentio's journey from Pisa could have been made, via the river Po, to Ostiglia, using the same canal route as Valentine and Proteus in *The Two Gentlemen of Verona*, but travelling in the opposite direction. Lucento would have taken his boat from Legnago, on the River Adige, to the Adriatic and then sailed the short distance northward to the Brenta River and on to Padua.

The indefatigable Mr Roe locates the exact spot at which Lucentio stands on arriving in Padua, with a square, a bridge over a waterway, a landing place and a street with the church of St Luke nearby. While much else has changed, the church of St Luke, where Bianca and Katherine were married, still stands in Padua today. From his vantage point in the square, Lucentio, standing in front of the hostelry in which he intends to stay, could chat with Tranio and at the same time call to Biondello, waiting in their boat at the landing stage below.

Once again the plot is entirely concerned with matrimony, and the stratagems young lovers use to mate with the girls of their dreams. We may assume that Marlowe was still living in northern Italy, probably in Verona or Padua, when he penned these plays.

With his facility in languages and his intimate knowledge of diplomacy, he would have had little difficulty in finding employment at the court of one of Italy's great princes, where he would have had access to libraries and writing materials, and he must have devised some means by which to send his completed scripts to England. Here again the contacts he had forged in Walsingham's employ would have been invaluable.

There is, as yet, no evidence that Marlowe lived in any specific place in Italy, but the circumstantial evidence for his having been familiar with several of its great cities is overwhelming. No one who had not visited Verona or Padua could have gleaned the intimate knowledge of the locale and the peculiar information known only to residents of those towns. So we may be fairly sure that Marlowe spent a good deal of time in the northern cities and very little in Rome or Naples or anywhere else.

One place that he must have known is Venice. Here again the sedulous Mr Roe has traced the footsteps of Portia and Shylock and other characters as they wend their way through the myriad waterways and pavements of the city. Roe was not a Marlovian, but he was convinced that whoever wrote the play must have had direct and personal knowledge of the towns of Northern Italy.

Talking of Shakespeare, Roe wrote:

> In the latter part of the sixteenth century,
> the gifted English playwright arrived in the
> beating heart of this Venetian empire: the
> legendary city of Venice. He moved about
> noting its structured society, its centuries-old
> government of laws, its traditions, its culture,
> and its disciplines. He carefully considered
> and investigated its engines of banking and
> commerce. He explored its harbours and
> canals, and its streets and squares. He saw the
> flash of its pageants, its parties and celebrations;
> and he looked deeply into the Venetian soul.
> Then, with a skill that has never been equalled,
> he wrote a story that has a happy ending for
> all its characters save one, about whom a grief
> endures and always will: a deathless tragedy.
>
> (Roe 115)

In *The Merchant of Venice*, Antonio, the merchant, begins the
play in solemn contemplation of his ships, some of which
are trading as far away as Mexico. Venetian ships were not
allowed to trade with Mexico, after Venice concluded a peace
treaty with the Ottoman Sultan in Turkey, for Philip of Spain
regarded this as anti-Christian and, accordingly, banned
all Venetian vessels from trading with his Spanish colonies.
Antonio, however, has his merchandise in foreign vessels,
namely in 'Argosies', the name given to ships from Ragosa,
the modern Dubrovnik, and he also uses an 'Andrew', a ship
owned by the wealthy Genoan family of Andrea Doria. One
wonders how Shakespeare of Stratford could have acquired
such a piece of information about Venetian laws and trading

without setting foot in Italy. The play abounds in evidence of such detailed knowledge and familiarity with local custom and practice.

Take, for instance, Bassanio's initial approach to Shylock, asking him for a loan so that he can court the wealthy Portia in the guise of a gentleman. Bassanio invites Shylock to dine with Antonio and himself, knowing full well that a Jew would never demean himself by eating a meal that was not kosher. Shylock replies with his acerbic statement: 'I will buy with you, sell with you, talk with you, walk with you, and so following: but I will not eat with you, drink with you, nor pray with you.' Shylock agrees to lend money which he intends to borrow from a friend of his, Tubal, whom he describes as being 'a wealthy Hebrew of my tribe'. This is not a tautology, but a reference to the fact that the Jewish community in Venice was divided into different sub-groups, according to their country of origin. Those of German origin were known as Ashkenazi. The next largest of these national groups were the Levantines, and then the Sephardic Jews, thrown out of Spain by order of Ferdinand and Isabella.

Roe sought, as always, to find the actual location of places mentioned in the text, and one he looked for, in particular, was the 'penthouse' where Shylock actually lived. The penthouse is mentioned by Gratiano, one of the young bloods who determine to harass Shylock by creating a disturbance under his window. Masked revellers were a common sight in Italian towns. Shylock dismisses them as: 'Christian fools with varnished faces'. Lorenzo, the lover of Shylock's daughter, Jessica, has planned a disturbance outside the house under cover of which he plans to entice her to elope. Gratiano remarks in the play (Act XI, sc. vi):

'This is the penthouse under which Lorenzo desired us make a stand.'

Once again, Roe tracks down the exact location, still there in the Ghetto in Venice today. It has a distinctive structure supported on three columns, which fits the definition of a penthouse, and it is the only such building of its kind in the Ghetto. It stands just a few yards from the Jewish museum.

As the action develops we learn that all of Antonio's Argosies have foundered, and Shylock is goaded beyond endurance by the insults and taunting of Antonio's friends. To make matters worse, his own daughter has run off with a Christian, taking with her his jewels and a precious ring given to him by his deceased wife. This ring, he is told, was exchanged by Jessica for a monkey. Shylock is distraught by this battery of misfortune, but his one consolation is the plight of Antonio, who has promised a pound of his own flesh if he fails to deliver payment in time. Shylock is determined 'to have his bond'.

Antonio is saved by the sagacity and erudition of Bassanio's wealthy heiress, Portia, who seeks the advice of a learned uncle, Belarius. To obtain his help, Portia sends Balthazar, a servant, to bring the requisite legal tomes back to Venice. Portia instructs him to meet her at the 'Tranect, the common ferry which trades to Venice'. Roe locates this as the point at which boats could transfer between the Venetian lagoon and the Brenta Canal. The Tranect was replaced in the following century by a pound lock.

It is typical of Roe's meticulous research that he locates the place so precisely. The same precision marks other references to specific places mentioned in the Italian plays. Take, for instance, the setting of Lucentio's speech on the quay at Padua, where half a dozen features of the townscape visible from the exact spot are mentioned by the playwright; or Helena's standing in Florence in the precise spot where she could see both the passing of Bertram's troops and the nunnery at which she lodged. Only one familiar with the local terrain, knowing Italy like the back of his hand, could draw on such effortless command of local topography.

It is, of course, important to remember that Roe never subscribed to the Marlovian thesis, but simply believed that Shakespeare had to have visited Italy and to have known it intimately, however, no Stratfordian scholar has yet adduced evidence that William of Stratford ever left England. For them, he is the omniscient genius, in no need of formal education or travel to broaden the mind, yet able to acquaint himself with the most minute details of life in France and Italy.

There has been much speculation over the location of Portia's Belmont, but here again Roe's painstaking research has left us with very little doubt. By piecing together the various references in the text, he comes to the conclusion that Belmont is the Villa Foscari-Malcontenta, constructed around 1560 and still in the hands of the Foscari family, now used as the central seat of the University of Venice. It has a timeless beauty, set among willows that overhang the Brenta Canal. Not far from here is the 'Tranect', the point at which the canal connects with the waters of the Venetian lagoon. It was probably some form of flash lock, as noted above replaced by a pound lock in later years, but it was at the Tranect that Portia and Nerissa made contact with Balthazar, and hence took from him the precious legal books to the courtroom in Venice.

When Portia makes her entrance to the courtroom, disguised as the learned young judge, she finds Shylock determined to exact the pound of Antonio's flesh that the merchant had so foolishly wagered. Antonio himself is apparently resigned to his fate, telling his friend Salanio:

1. Canterbury Cathedral where Marlowe sang as a boy chorister and later studied at the neighbouring Queen's School.

2. The tower of the church of St George the Martyr, where Marlowe was christened in February 1564. The church was destroyed by enemy action in 1942, together with the house nearby in which the Marlowe family lived.

3. Ruins of Scadbury Castle, the home of Thomas Walsingham, in a country park near Chislehurst in Kent, where Marlowe was arrested in May 1593. There is nothing left of interest above ground level. The chimneys are whimsical additions by a wealthy owner in the 1930s.

4. The moat still surrounds the site as it did in Walsingham's day.

Photographed by courtesy of the Orpington and District Archaeological Society.

5. *Nonsuch* Palace by Georg Hoefnagel,1558. It was built by a jubilant Henry VIII to celebrate the birth of his son, Prince Edward, but was demolished by the Countess of Castlemaine, mistress of Charles II, in 1682 to pay her gambling debts.

6. A model of the palace created by Mr Ben Taggart, in 2011, under the direction of Professor Martin Biddle, who conducted the first modern excavation of the site in 1959.

7. Nothing remains of the palace today, but the foundations of this contemporaneous banqueting house can still be seen just a short distance from the site.

8. Shylock's penthouse in the Jewish quarter of Venice, the only building that fits the description in the Ghetto, just a few yards from the Jewish museum.

9. Portia's Belmont, the Villa Foscari-Malcontenta, designed by Andrea Palladio (1549–63) on the Brenta Canal, now the central seat of the University of Venice.

10. St Luke's church in Padua, where Katherine and Bianca were married in *The Taming of the Shrew*.

11. The Porta Palio, one of the western gates of Verona, through which sycamore trees can still be seen. It was here that Benvolio tells Romeo's mother that he had seen Romeo walking an hour before daybreak.

12. Sycamores growing outside the Porta Palio today. They are growing, with other varieties, on a spacious traffic island beyond the city walls.

13. Villafranca, the great castle of Prince Escalus, near Verona, to which he summoned old Montague for judgement in *Romeo and Juliet*.

14. Piazza Erbe, showing the southern side of the Scaliger Palace, in Verona. Scaliger is derived from the name Escalus.

15. Juliet's balcony, placed here in the 1930s, by a canny local authority, to satisfy the demands of tourists.

16. The house of Romeo, utterly ignored by most tourists, close to the Scaliger Palace in Verona. The much defaced plaque includes the familiar misquotation 'Romeo, Romeo, Where art thou Romeo?'

17. Entrance to the monastery of St Francis, where Romeo and Juliet were married.

18. The supposed tomb of Juliet in the Capulet vault of the Franciscan monastery.

19. Testifying to the universal appeal of the 'tale of such woe', a modern sculpture by a Chinese artist.

20. A map of the city walls of Sabbioneta, the putative location of *A Midsummer Night's Dream*.

21. The walls of Sabbioneta, 'little Athens', the perfect medieval fortified city, a magnet to artists and philosophers, created by Vespasiano Gonzaga who died in 1591.

22. Another view of the walls, showing the other entrance resembling a Roman gateway.

23. Another part of the wall that surrounds Sabbioneta.

24. Port della Vittoria, also known as 'the Duke's Oak' since it once led to an oak forest which was the Duke's hunting ground.

25. Church of the Crowned Virgin, known as 'the temple' to which Vespasiano added his own mausoleum.

26. Monument to Vespasiano Gonzaga, in his mausoleum attached to the temple.

27. Beneath the long gallery, built to house the Duke's collection of antiquities.

28. The long gallery, 96 metres in length, that once held the Duke's collection of Roman statuary. The collection was dispersed after his death.

29. The auditorium of the first purpose-built theatre in the world, built by Vespasiano in the 1570s.

30. A model of the theatre of Sabbioneta. Apparently this stage set was adapted for any production.

31. The Porta Romana, Florence, from which Bertram would have marched as he returned from the Florentine Wars in *All's Well that Ends Well.*

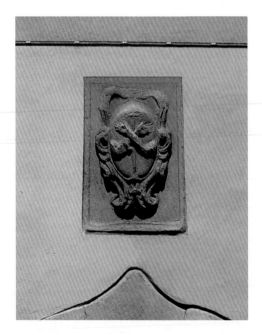

32. The sign of St Francis, in the wall above a doorway of the pilgrim's hostel where Helen stayed in Florence. The plaque shows the crucified hand of Christ crossing that of St Francis, with its stigmata.

> The Duke cannot deny the course of law;
> For the commodity that strangers have
> With us in Venice, if it be denied,
> Will much impeach the justice of the state,
> Since that the trade and profit of the city
> Consisteth of all nations.

Act III, sc. iii, lines 2–31

In other words, the prosperity of Venice depended on strict observance of mercantile law, and if Antonio had been so foolish as to pledge his own flesh as surety for the bond, then the penalty must be exacted, according to the terms agreed. Portia's pleading with Shylock to accept payment, and her impassioned speech about the quality of mercy, fall on deaf ears. It is only when she seizes on a specific aspect of the bond, the fact that it makes no mention of shedding blood, that the tide turns, and it turns viciously against Shylock.

The trial scene is pure theatre, written for English audiences. It bears little relation to the actual conduct and interpretation of the law by a Venetian court, but it leaves us deeply aware of the injustices done to Jews like Shylock. Marlowe must have lived and worked close to the mercantile community in Italy and his sympathies, like ours, can only have rested with the dejected figure of an old man, abused and derided, deceived and abandoned by his only child, and beaten into the ground by his enemies.

If Marlowe was employed by the Medici or some other powerful family, it is likely that he would be free to travel and explore the countryside, as well as the great cities of Tuscany, Lombardy and the Veneto. It is possible that, like Roe, he happened to find himself staying for a while in the little town of Sabbioneta, a few miles southwest of Mantua.

Sabbioneta was a model city built to the order of its wealthy and enlightened duke, Vespasiano Gonzaga Colonna, who lived from 1531 to 1591. As a young man, Vespasiano was sent to the court of Philip II of Spain. He won great honours as a military man and as an architect devoted to the Roman writer, Vitruvius, author of *De Architectura*. The whole of Sabbioneta was designed by the Duke, and the city was coterminous with his ducal palace. It was a masterpiece of renaissance planning and it attracted visitors from far and wide. Supposing one of these happened to be Christopher Marlowe, then it is very likely he wrote his delightful play based on precisely what the title says: a midsummer night's dream.

When Roe visited there it was simply as a tourist, with no thought of finding more evidence of Shakespeare's travels but, quite by chance, he discovered what appears to have been the location of *A Midsummer Night's Dream*, set not in the Athens of Greece, but in this small town, known as 'little Athens', because its ruler, Vespasiano Gonzaga, deliberately attracted scholars and intellectuals to live there. According to James Madge in his book *Sabbioneta Cryptic City*, one of the regular visitors to the court at Sabbioneta was Bernadino Baldi 'who spoke twelve languages and was among the first to take an interest in Etruscan antiquities'. Baldi also wrote a number of books on architecture and devised a large-scale solar clock. Other visitors to the court were Marcello Donati, who started a botanical garden, and a musician, Carlo Magnanimi, as well as legal experts, mathematicians, astronomers, historians and poets.

What alerted Roe to his discovery was the mention of 'the Duke's Oak', which is, of course, the place where the rustic troupe of actors − Bottom the weaver, Quince, the carpenter, Snug the joiner, Flute, the bellows-maker, Snout, the tinker and Starveling, the tailor − agree to meet in order to rehearse their play. The Duke's Oak was not a tree but the name given to the main gate of the city.

One other specific reference confirms the city as the location of the play, namely the mention of the 'temple' where the duke bids the company to attend him for the marriage of the lovers. This 'temple' was in fact the church next to the mausoleum of Vespasiano Gonzaga. It was officially called 'The Church of the Crowned Virgin', but it was more commonly known simply as 'the temple'.

It is generally understood that the last of the great plays was *The Tempest*. It is seen as the writer's own farewell to his literary career, perhaps because he was getting tired or running out of ideas, but if there is a consensus about the placing of the play in the canon, there is precious little in speculation as to its geographical location. Commentators have placed it somewhere in the West Indies or the Isle of Man, but, once again, Roe finds its exact location in Italy, on a small island off the northern shore of Sicily, in the Tyrrhenian Sea, the island of Vulcano.

There is, however, a difficulty in the route that Prospero and his infant daughter are said to have taken in order to complete their sea voyage, borne by the currents, for Prospero claims to have been ejected by his brother from Milan. If this were so, the currents would have taken them into the Adriatic, on the eastern side of the Italian landmass. Roe suggests that the playwright might have originally given Florence as their point of departure, enabling them to go by the River Arno and thence by canal to the port of Livorno. He suggests that this distortion from the obvious route was made in order to avoid offending the Florentines, with whom England was engaged in profitable trade. Milan, on the other hand, was under Habsburg control and it would have been of little consequence if the play caused offence to the authorities there.

As a student of Virgil, Marlowe was well aware that the route taken in *The Tempest* by King Alonso, from Tunis to Naples, was identical to that taken by Aeneas some 1,500 years earlier. The story of Aeneas and his forlorn lover, Queen Dido, was the subject of one of Marlowe's very first plays, *Dido, Queen of Carthage*. Marlowe's intimate knowledge of the *Aeneid* would have made him fully aware of the parallel between the perils inflicted by Prospero and those visited on Aeneas by Aeolus, god of the winds. Juno appealed to him to raise up a storm against Aeneas:

> Hammer your winds to fury and ruin their swamped ships, or scatter them and fling their crews piecemeal across the seas.
>
> *Aeneid*, Book I, quoted by Roe 275

When he turned his attention to Denmark and the great tragedy of *Hamlet*, the playwright returned, in the players' scene, to this same story of Dido and Aeneas. Hamlet asks the first player to give a 'taste of his quality' by reciting a particular speech, from 'Aeneas' tale to Dido ... where he speaks of Priam's slaughter'. Thus 'Shakespeare' in his most mature play offers homage to the first of his own creations, as a young dramatist, by singling out a passage from *Dido, Queen of Carthage* to be performed by the players. He appears to be saying that the play was not popular, but that, in his personal opinion, it had a good deal of merit:

Hamlet   I heard thee speak me a speech once, but it was never acted, or, if it was, not above once; for the play, I remember, pleased not the million. 'Twas caviare to the general. But it was – as I received it, and others whose judgements in such matters cried in the top of mine – an excellent play, well digested in the scenes, set down with as much modesty as cunning. I remember one said there were no sallets in the lines to make the matter savoury, nor no matter in the phrase that might indict the author of affectation, but called it an honest method, as wholesome as sweet, and by very much more handsome than fine.

Hamlet, Act II, sc. ii, lines 436–47

The lines spoken in *Hamlet* are not to be found in Marlowe's early play, but they are close to its style and subject matter, and might well have been inspired by the writer's memory of his early play, *Dido, Queen of Carthage* (Act II, sc. ii).

Of all the cities of Italy most likely to appeal to the urbane and cultured Marlowe, Florence would surely have offered the greatest attraction. He did not, however, choose to set his plays there, except for one scene in *All's Well that Ends Well*. The play revolves around Bertram's haughty disdain of the virtuous Helena. He rejects her, saying: 'I'll to the Tuscan wars and never bed her' (Act II, sc. iii, 270). In his absence, Helena engineers the 'bed trick' in which he makes love to her believing she is a common prostitute.

When Bertram returns from the wars to Florence, he comes to the great Porta Romana, and then marches with his men northward through the city. Crossing the Arno by the Ponte alla Carraia, he passes the Piazza Goldoni. Near this spot, Helena watches him, dressed as a pilgrim. She asks a poor widow where a pilgrim, like herself, should seek lodging. The widow answers: 'At the "Saint Francis" here beside the port'. With his phenomenal grasp of history and his unerring gift in detecting the precise locations in the plays, Roe identifies the very house, with its symbol of Saint

Francis still embedded in the wall above a doorway, on the Borgo Ognissanti.

Only one familiar with the very detailed topography of Florence could conceivably have registered the existence of this sign, above the doorway of the hostel in which Helen stayed. Marlowe must indeed have known Italy intimately. This was the opinion of Professor Ernesto Grillo, whose book, *Shakespeare and Italy*, appeared posthumously in 1949. Grillo was confident that not only 'must Shakespeare have visited Italy', but that he 'must have visited Milan, Verona, Venice, Padua and Mantua'. In *The Merchant of Venice*, says Grillo, 'the topography is so precise and accurate that it must convince even the most superficial reader that the poet visited the country, accurately observant of all its characteristics'.

8

Local Colour

However much the culture and customs of Italy suited Marlowe, he would surely have felt homesick for England. Yet there could be no return from the dead without endangering all those who were party to, or cognisant of, the original deception, so any return would have to be strictly incognito, perhaps to discuss the publishing of his sonnets or new plays with Thomas Thorpe. In 1609, Thorpe put together an edition of Shakspeare's sonnets. It appears to have been suppressed almost immediately, possibly at the behest of Thomas Walsingham, for fear that the poems might reveal the truth about Marlowe's disappearance. There were so few copies of the sonnets printed, that as late as 1640 they were published as previously unknown poems by Shakespeare.

Earlier, in 1600, Thorpe may have attempted to publish *As You Like It*, but if so, the play was 'stayed' or suppressed, probably, again to protect Walsingham. Nevertheless, Thorpe was jubilant at having in his possession so great a literary scoop, boasting to Edmund Blount, who was later to be one of the printers of the First Folio, that he had something that would surprise him. As Blount was a friend of Walsingham, it was doubtless Blount who had the play suppressed. The reason for this we will examine later, but it is Thomas Thorpe's letter which is of immediate interest, for in it he gives a heavy hint that Marlowe, whom he describes as 'that pure elemental wit', is still alive and in London at that time. His 'ghost or Genius is to be seen walk the Churchyard in (at the least) three or four sheets'. The 'Churchyard' refers to St Paul's churchyard where new works were authorised at the Stationers' Hall, the 'three or four sheets' may well refer to the disguise adopted by Marlowe. He could have assumed the identity of a Berber covered in long flowing robes.

Why should *As You Like It* have been suppressed? It was not alone to receive the censure of the Lord Chamberlain – *Henry IV, Much Ado* etc. were also disallowed, but they were performed a few years later. Only this comedy was denied approval until it appeared in the edition of 1623. The explanation surely is that its covert references to the true author and his fate might be revealed. Walsingham could not allow this to happen.

In the play, Touchstone, the clown, takes a fancy to Audrey, a young shepherdess. She already has an admirer in the shape of William of Arden, but Touchstone tells him in no uncertain terms to leave Audrey alone. The most perplexing speech comes after Touchstone has asked William: 'Art thou learned?' to which he confesses, 'No, sir.' Touchstone replies:

> Then learn this of me: to have, is to have.
> For it is a figure in rhetoric, that drink, being poured
> out of a cup into a glass, by filling the one doth empty
> the other. For all your writers do consent that ipse is
> he. Now you are not ipse, for I am he.
> Act IV, sc. i, lines 40–43

This speech may be construed as being penned by Marlowe and addressed to William Shakespeare. The meaning would seem to be, I am the true author of the works issued in your name and I am no longer prepared to suffer your insolence.

'Audrey' conjours the notion of audience, or the theatre-going public. The cup and glass analogy indicates that they cannot both receive credit for the plays. 'Touchstone' is also a word meaning an indicator of the truth, used by medieval alchemists to reveal the purity of gold. To test a metal's purity, the object had to make physical contact with the touchstone. It is only when William gives his hand to Touchstone that he is exposed as a fool.

Touchstone then launches into a virulent attack upon William, telling him to leave the society of this woman, that is, stop pretending to be the author of my works or I shall 'kill thee, make thee away, translate thy life into death, thy liberty into bondage, I will deal in poison with thee ... I will kill thee a hundred and fifty ways. Therefore tremble, and depart' (Act V, sc. i, lines 45–56). How might Marlowe have carried out this threat to expose William as a fraud? He could not; not without bringing vengeance upon the whole group of conspirators that had made possible his departure from Deptford. But if he were to publish his roughly 150 sonnets, the truth might well be discerned.

There is a further reference to Marlowe's fate in the play. It occurs in a conversation between Audrey and Touchstone where Touchstone says:

> When a man's verses cannot be understood,
> nor a man's good wit seconded with the forward child
> understanding, it strikes a man more dead than a great
> reckoning in a little room.
>
> Act III, sc. iii, lines 7–12

It is a passage that might well have evoked memories of Marlowe's own fate, struck dead in a fight over payment of a paltry bill in a small room. In fact, the reference would probably have meant little to anyone but Marlowe at the time, for it was not until the coroner's report was discovered by Leslie Hotson in 1925 that the significance of the phrase was explained.

If Thorpe had indeed caught sight of Marlowe in 1600, it is most unlikely that he stayed for any length of time in England. The risk of discovery was appreciated not only by Marlowe himself, but by the whole coterie of his friends. Raleigh had enemies, as did most men at court, and Archbishop Whitgift was still determined to root out heresy. The rack was still used to extract information from Catholic priests, as well as extreme Protestants and suspected traitors.

Marlowe may have spent some time in Scotland, preparing his Scottish tragedy, or perhaps visiting Denmark to familiarise himself with its people and history, before working on the story of *Hamlet*. In all probability, he returned before long to Italy, the country in which most of his plays were set apart from the histories. But he continued to find inspiration for drama in the story of England's kings.

The trilogy concerning Henry VI was, for many years, attributed to Marlowe rather than Shakespeare, which, alone, is supportive of our argument that Marlowe and Shakespeare are one and the same. It is probable that the three plays were completed before he left England in 1593. *Richard II* and *Richard III* both saw the light of day in 1597 and the two parts of *Henry IV* and *Henry V* were printed between 1598 and 1600. *King John* appears to have been a late play, printed in 1611, and *Henry VIII* is regarded as Shakespeare's very last play which was playing at The Globe when it was engulfed by flames in 1613.

The Merry Wives of Windsor is connected to the history plays only by the character of Falstaff, whom the Queen is reputed to have enjoyed so much that she desired to see a play about the fat knight in love. It is worth noting that one of the central incidents in the play, in which Falstaff is hidden in a laundry basket and unceremoniously dumped in the river, may have its origin in a story that would have been circulating in Canterbury when Marlowe was at school. Dr William Urry came across it in the archives of the Library and Dean of the Chapter of Canterbury, and it is quoted by Mrs Wraight in her book, *The Story the Sonnets Tell* as follows:

> At about harvest time in 1575, one Goodwife Thomasina Newen went round to the Northgate ward of Canterbury to the house of Goodwife Pratt, and sat working with her at her door. Near by a new-made widow, Goodwife Culverhouse, gave milk to her child. They gossiped of Clemence Ward, saying 'Yt is a pity she is not carted out of town.' One story which they told about her was repeated a few months later with slight variations in the kitchen of the house of Goodwife Joan Moyse, a widow and 'impotent woman' aged fifty, when Clemence Ward's landlord, John Foster, kindly went to see if Goodwife Moyse lacked for anything. As Goodwife Moyse rambled on, retelling a story told previously by a Mrs Hunt, as she recalled, she conjured up a scene of two people staggering through Christchurch Gate into the cathedral precincts on the way to Canon Darrell's house at the far east end, by the city wall, carrying between them a laundry basket over which a coverlet was spread. They went along the great length of the 'Centuary', or cemetery of Canterbury Cathedral, through the Norman gateway to

the inner cemetery until they came to the Oaks in front of Canon Darrell's house. There they set the basket down, in among the oak trees. The laundry basket was going, said Goodwife Lea, 'to Mr Darrell's chamber'. Before long either Mr Whyting or perhaps Mr Wade, one of the cathedral lay clerks, approached with some foreknowledge of what was in the basket. He drew out his dagger and plunged it into the basket and, with a wound in her arm from the dagger, out leapt Clemence Ward.

> William Urry, *Christopher Marlowe and Canterbury*, posthumously edited by Andrew Butcher (1988) 34-35, and quoted by Wraight, 326

Mrs Wraight notes that the story emanates from a time when Marlowe was aged 11 and a chorister at the cathedral. The scandal could not have escaped the young Marlowe's ears and may well have influenced his opinion of clerical morality. We know that Marlowe was active in the unearthing of Catholic plots against the Queen, although he probably learned to respect the Roman Church during his long sojourn in Italy. Several writers have suggested he was a secret Catholic himself, notably Clare Asquith in *Shadowplay* (Public Affairs, 2005). Marlowe's portrayal of Malvolio in *Twelfth Night* shows a decided lack of sympathy with Puritanism. 'Dost thou think,' Sir Toby asks Malvolio, 'because thou art virtuous there shall be no more cakes and ale?' When Maria says he is 'sometimes a kind of puritan', Sir Andrew Aguecheek replies: 'O, if I thought that I'd beat him like a dog' and Maria remarks, 'The dev'l a puritan that he is, or anything constantly but a time-pleaser, an affectioned ass that cons state without book and utters it by great swathes' (Act II, sc. iii, lines 110–43).

Marlowe had sufficient love for his native land to be able to recreate its fields and woodlands in his mind's eye. He had also acquired a fund of stories, like the salacious gossip surrounding Canon Darell and the laundry basket, that provided material for his dramatic imagination in *The Merry Wives*. Another piece of gossip from his home town concerned a love affair conducted through a hole in a garden wall. The *dramatis personae* in this case were Dorothy Hocking and Richard Edmundes. Dorothy led a miserable life as the domestic slave of her step-parents, who kept her under strict surveillance. Dorothy contrived to join her hand to that of Richard through a hole in the garden wall. Holding her hand, Richard stated: 'well my wench I beare youe good will and if thow canst find in thie harte to love me and wilbe ruled by me I will delyver thee out of thye miserie'. Dorothy having made the necessary commitment to love him above all other, witnesses were called to their plighting their troth, 'through the hole in the wall'. The similarity between this case from the Canterbury archives and the rustics' play of *Pyramus and Thisbe* is immediately apparent (Act V, scene I, lines 153–200).

Many attempts have been made to fix Shakespeare's boyhood to places mentioned in the plays without a deal of success, but some locations would certainly have been more familiar to the young Marlowe than to a man from Warwickshire – for example, the scene so vividly conjured by Edgar in *King Lear* where he leads the blind Duke of Gloucester, his father, to the cliff edge and describes for him what he sees when looking over the imagined edge:

> Come on sir; here's the place. Stand still. How fearful
> And dizzy 'tis to cast one's eyes so low!
> The crows and choughs that wing the mid-way air
> Show scarce so gross as beetles. Half-way down

Hangs one that gathers samphire – dreadful trade!
Methinks he seems no bigger than his head.
The fishermen that walk upon the beach
Appear like mice; and yon tall anchoring bark
Diminish'd to her cock; her cock, a bouy
Almost too small for sight. The murmuring surge
That on th'unnumb'red idle pebble chafes
Cannot be heard so high. I'll look no more;
Lest my brain turn, and the deficient sight
Topple down headlong.

King Lear, Act IV, sc. vi, lines 11–24

There are numerous other references to Kent and the Kentish countryside in the *Henry VI* trilogy and in *Henry IV* which would have occurred naturally to the man born in Canterbury, but which one would not expect from a native of Stratford upon Avon – for example, the robbery at Gadshill, a village not far from Canterbury. Another reference to a village close to Canterbury has been identified by William Urry, in *Henry IV* part II, where one character cries: 'I see them, I see them! There's Best's son, the tanner of Wingham.' Peter Farey explains the connexion thus:

'Christopher Marlowe's father was a shoemaker. Just three and a half miles to the east of his shop – and a couple of miles before the road reaches Wingham – was a tannery where the road crossed the Nail Bourne. One and a half miles down a road to the right of this is Bekesbourne. It is there that on 19th March 1582, Joseph Best, the son of John Best, was baptised and one may reasonably assume that he was a brother to Thomas Best, also baptised in Bekesbourne, some three years earlier on 22nd February 1579. So both Wingham and a Best family are known to have been within a couple of miles of a tannery which was very probably used by Marlowe's father.'

9

The First Night of Twelfth Night

It is unlikely that Marlowe would have lingered long in London in 1600, when Blount spoke of seeing him in St Paul's churchyard, for the danger of discovery was still very real. But, by 1601, we have reason to believe he did return, though of course under an assumed name. This was to oversee the production of *Twelfth Night* in a private showing before Her Majesty.

Precisely what work he found during his years in Italy we do not know, but it seems probable that by the end of the decade, if not earlier, Marlowe was in the service of Don Virginio Orsino, Duke of Bracciano. Virginio was a highly cultured man, about ten years younger than Marlowe, who would have been impressed by the talents of the émigré Englishman, with his command of languages and knowledge of the world.

Virginio's uncle was the Grand Duke Ferdinand of Tuscany. This was the same man depicted in Webster's play, *The White Devil*, who strangled his wife, when Orsino was just 4 years old. He later murdered the husband of Vittoria Acorambona, with whom he was infatuated. His political ambition was to free his country from the domination of Spain, and although he had been obliged to provide a ship for the Armada against England, Ferdinand was delighted with the outcome of that enterprise.

In 1589, the year after the Armada, Duke Ferdinand married the French princess, Christine of Lorraine, and also arranged a match between Don Virginio and Flavia Peretti, the grand niece of Pope Sixtus V, who provided her with a dowry of 100,000 crowns. This papal matchmaking also presented an occasion to reconcile two rival families, the Orsini and the Colonna. Sixtus ruled that whichever had the elder in age should have precedence, but that in all other respects they were equal and should outrank all other Roman barons.

Flavia soon bore two children, a boy and a girl twins, and before he was 29 Virginio had six children. He acquitted himself well in fighting the Turkish armies in Hungary but was less successful in an attempt to liberate the island of Chios in 1599. By this time, Phillip of Spain had been succeeded by his son and the Pope had died, to be followed by Pope Clement VIII. Relations between the new Pope and the Orsinis were predictably strained, as they were with the new papal envoy, Cardinal Aldobrandini.

In 1600, Grand Duke Ferdinand engineered the marriage of his niece, Maria de Medici, with Henry of Navarre, an event that occasioned the most lavish of celebrations at the Palazzo Pitti, the Tuscan court of the Grand Duke. Anxious to show his supremacy over the Orsinis, the Pope sent Cardinal Aldobrandini to represent him at the nuptials, with a grand display of papal wealth. Remembering the decree of Pope Sixtus, giving precedence over other Roman barons, the Grand Duke and his nephew, Don Virginio, rode out of the Porta Romana to greet the papal legate. As a special sign of his beneficence the Pope sent a sanctified emblem, the Golden Rose, and Don Virginio was assigned to carry this precious emblem before the procession.

Ettiquette on such occasions was of the utmost importance,

and Aldobrandino was specifically told to assert his pre-eminence by riding at the head of the procession, in order to humiliate the Orsinis, showing them that the new Pope had overridden the decree of his predecessor. Don Virginio was apprised of the plan and simply ignored the Pope's wishes. Instead he rode out ahead of the Cardinal. It was a major snub to the Vatican and Virginio made it clear that it was no accident. In resolute terms, he sent to tell the Cardinal that 'he, Orsino, was at Florence, and not at Rome, and that, even in Rome, he would never have submitted' to the new decree. Aldobrandino was so incensed that he turned back to Rome and refused to officiate at the marriage. To this, the Grand Duke's bastard brother replied that 'every priest was sufficient to do the same business he came for' (letter from John Hanam in Florence to Sir John Popham, the Lord Chief Justice, quoted in Hotson, *The First Night of Twelfth Night*, 53).

We might pause here and take a closer look at this bastard brother of the Duke. He is the same character as we meet in *Much Ado About Nothing*. The sinister presence of Don John pervades the whole of that play, from his apologetic introduction to the ducal party to the final scene, in which he is denounced and promised suitable punishment by Benedict. In his eagerness to destroy the honour and happiness of the young bride, Hero, and to create discord wherever possible, he reminds one of Iago in *Othello*. He is the embodiment of evil, but we cannot even warm to his wit.

The real-life Don John (1547–78) was the bastard brother of Philip II of Spain. According to Roe, he was the illegitimate son of the Holy Roman Emperor Charles V, who was also King of Spain from 1519 to 1556. Two years before his death, Charles handed his throne and his empire to his only legitimate son, Philip. Thereafter John, who was almost certainly superior to his brother in ability, had to defer to whatever Philip chose to allow him to do. Already a seasoned naval commander, he won great acclaim for his victory in the Battle of Lepanto, in 1571, saving Christendom from the power of the Turkish fleet. It was a resounding victory. Don John had proved himself fit to rule and yearned for a crown of his own. There was open talk of his becoming King of England if and when Mary Stuart ascended the throne. Even before Lepanto, Pope Pius V had dreamed of an invasion of England with the object of assassinating Elizabeth and putting Mary Stuart on the throne, with Don John as her husband. With this in view, Pius excommunicated Elizabeth early in 1571. But Philip did not favour the idea, and John's hopes came to nothing. It would appear that, for all his talents, or because of them, John became a classic figure of hate in England. He was indelibly marked as a foreign threat and a demonic figure to every true Englishman.

Virginio showed no sign of remorse for offending the Pope and instead he began to add further offence by planning to visit the Pope's arch enemy, Queen Elizabeth. There had already been contact between the two courts earlier in the year, when William Cecil, heir to Lord Burleigh and nephew of the Queen's first minister, Robert Cecil, was entertained at the Pitti Palace by Don Virginio. However, for a nominally Catholic prince to pay a visit to the excommunicant Queen was something of a different order. The journey had to be performed with the utmost discretion and secrecy.

Elizabeth could not fail to welcome a Tuscan alliance, which enraged the Spaniards. She was gratified, too, at a marriage that put a Medici on the throne of France rather than a Spanish nominee. A visit from Virginio might also open the treasure chest of his uncle, the wealthiest man in Europe. Elizabeth apparently told her agent in France to suggest to Ferdinand that he might contribute to her war-chest 'as one that hath the best power to bear part of the charges, and most cause to suspect the greatness of Spayne'.

Ralph Winwood, the English agent in Florence, wrote to Sir Henry Neville from Lyons, on 20 November, that Virginio made a show of departing from France after depositing Maria de Medici, but that in fact he 'came disguised to Avignon' en route to England and the Low Countries. Hotson suggests the letter from Winwood arrived in London around 10 December and that this was the first intimation anyone had of his imminent visit. His actual arrival was on Christmas Day 1600. Leslie Hotson describes in detail the preparations for the entertainment of Virginio and especially the plans to stage a new 'Shakespeare' play, *Twelfth Night, or What You Will* at the palace of Westminster in front of the Queen and Don Virginio on 6 January 1601. This was, Hotson claims, the first night of *Twelfth Night*.

The play is so obviously written for this specific event, yet no one was even aware of Virginio's presence in England until two weeks before the play was to be performed. How can it possibly be imagined that any writer could produce such an exquisite masterpiece in so short a time? It stretches the bounds of credulity too far to imagine William Shakespeare settling down to write and produce the play, with all its allusions to the honoured guest of the Queen, with a deadline less than two weeks from the earliest date of its commissioning. Christopher Marlowe, on the other hand, most probably had wind of Don Virginio's plans from the outset. He may well have acted as a courier to the royal party, as an experienced multilingual traveller, and he would have had ample time to write a fitting tribute to both his Italian employer and the Queen of England.

Hotson has the most vivid descriptions of the setting, the stage furnishings, the seating arrangements and the reaction of the guests, including the Russian Ambassador, Boris Gudunov. He goes on to describe the intimate conversations and entertainments laid on at court and the way in which Elizabeth and her younger guest danced through the night, evidently entranced with each other's company.

The very idea that such a play was composed and written out for public performance by a jobbing actor, or indeed anyone in England within a fortnight, is preposterous. The writer of *Twelfth Night* had to have known of the projected visit well in advance and to have had time to write a play specifically related to the two individuals in the audience, mirrored in so many ways by the main characters. Marlowe had probably been employed by the Duke of Bracciano for several months, or even years, prior to the visit to England and it is highly likely that he had a hand in planning the route and that he was there in the great hall of Whitehall Palace to put the final touches to his play and to supervise the whole performance.

Hotson reprints correspondence of Ralph Winwood, with Sir Henry Neville, Ambassador to Henry of Navarre, who was in London at the time, concerning the proposed journey. On the day after the wedding, Winwood wrote from Lyons: 'I have been entreated by a gentleman who doth accompany Don Virginio into England (whereof in my letter of the 20th of November I advertised) to address them by some letter to someone who would vouchsafe to make them have the sight of the Court, and access to Her Majesty. I have given them a letter to your Lordship' (Hotson, *The First Night of Twelfth Night*, 63).

Don Virginio had four travelling companions, including a 'secretary', and it is quite conceivable that this was, in fact, Marlowe in disguise. The party arrived in England on 25 December 1600.

In looking at the play, Hotson identifies Malvolio as Sir William Knollys, Comptroller of the Queens Household. He was responsible for keeping all her household servants in order and, consequently, fair game as the butt of the revellers' pranks. Knollys was a cousin once removed to Queen Elizabeth, his grandmother being Mary Bullen. He was a thoroughgoing Puritan, from Banbury in Oxfordshire, which was renowned for its persecution of tinkers, as well as for its disapproval of dancing and other popular entertainments, such as bear-baiting. Knollys was, at the time, the subject of much ribald comment for the attention he was paying to a young lady at court, named Mary Fitton. Five years earlier Mary Fitton had become one of the Queen's ladies in waiting, in the care of Knollys.

Despite his role as her guardian, Knollys was soon begging her to marry him as soon as his wife had died. Fitton had no difficulty in repulsing a man 21 years her senior, but she did fall for the young William, Lord Herbert, later Earl of Pembroke. She evidently strayed beyond wise limits in her relationship, as a son was born to her, out of wedlock, and her public disgrace followed.

Knollys personifies hostility to hilarity and misrule, '*mala-voglia*', but the words can also be seen as a 'sly modulation' of '*Mal-voglio*' which means 'I want Mal' or mistress Mary Fitton. The jest is compounded by reference to his yellow stockings which alludes to a popular song at the time:

> When I was a bachelor I led a merry life;
> But now I am a married man, and troubled with a wife ...
> Give me my yellow hose again, give me my yellow hose!
> For now my wife she watcheth me: see yonder where she goes!

> Hotson 106

Hotson tells us that Queen Elizabeth abhorred yellow, the flag of her arch enemy, Spain. It was also the proper wear for jealous husbands. The English byword for jealousy was 'to wear yellow stockings and cross garters', the latter being a fashion 'chiefly worn by old men, Puritans, pedants, footmen, and rustic bridegrooms'.

But the jokes at Malvolio's expense are part of the comic sub-plot; the main story concerns the attempts of Duke Orsino to court the lovely Lady Olivia, who is grieving for the loss of her dead brother. It is not difficult to see Elizabeth in the character of Olivia, rejecting the overtures of young lovers and the object of universal admiration. The similarities between fictional and real-life characters are noticeable. Orsino bears the same name and is greatly fond of music. They were both the fathers of twins, though in real life the Duke had five more children. Orsino is 'learned and valiant' as was Don Virginio. Marlowe will have known about these traits and peculiar characteristics and so wove them into his plot, to the delight of his Florentine master and his royal companion in the audience. But he could not linger in London for fear of discovery by his enemies.

Silence over the affair at Deptford was still essential to the well-being of Marlowe's erstwhile companions, but it is also clear from the story of *Twelfth Night* that the truth must have been known to a significant number of people close to and including the Queen. We can only speculate that Marlowe returned to Florence with Don Virginio. They left London on 13 January and took a boat from Dover to Calais a few days later.

Marlowe, the ex-spy and secret agent, was probably well-versed in arts of disguise, and we may speculate that Marlowe is likely to have returned to England on several more occasions.

He may well have seen some of his plays, attributed to William Shakespeare, but performed under his own direction, especially if they were also acted at the Queen's command, as was surely the case with *The Merry Wives of Windsor*.

10

Unmasking the Man

If we read the sonnets as reflecting his own journey into exile, we may also see in many of his plays a reflection of Marlowe's spiritual journey. Hamlet is a prince deprived of his rightful place and forced to remain in the shadows, incapable of coming out into the open. In *Lear*, again we have main characters deprived of their birthright and obliged to remain incognito, disguised for fear of identification. Disguise is a common feature in most of the plays: Rosalind in *As You Like It*, Julia in *The Two Gentlemen*, Portia in *The Merchant*, the pranksters at Gadshill in *Henry IV*, the courtly jesters in *Love's Labour's Lost*, the multiple changes of costume in *Cymbeline* and the transformation of Bottom in the *Dream*.

Stephen Greenblatt notes: 'the peculiar intensity with which Shakespeare repeatedly embraces the fantasy of the recovery of a lost prosperity or title or identity is striking'. 'Again and again' he writes, 'an unforeseen catastrophe ... turns what has seemed like happy progress, prosperity, smooth sailing, into disaster, terror and loss ... this catastrophe is often epitomized by the deliberate alteration or disappearance of the name and, with it, the alteration or disappearance of social status' – as with Valentine in *The Two Gentlemen of Verona*.

Much of this adoption of different appearance can be explained by the convention that prevented women from

89

acting on the stage, but the necessity for staying out of sight, and constantly having to assume another guise, may explain why mistaken identity and the adoption of different personae appear so often in the plays.

It may well be asked, why should the great deception have lasted so long? Why after Shakespeare and Marlowe were dead, did the truth about their relationship not emerge? The answer would seem to be that even after many of the characters were dead, there were some who feared exposure for their part in the deception. The Church was still powerful in the prosecution of heretics and had control over what was published. Too many people had been party to the fraud who would not wish their names to be associated with the scandalous reprobate that Marlowe had become in popular belief. Writers were still liable to be called to account for alluding to matters of state. Ben Jonson's *Sejanus*, about a Roman general in the time of Tiberius, was thought to be an allusion to the trial of Raleigh and therefore seditious. Jonson was summoned to the Privy Council in 1605. The previous year he was jailed for his part in a play called *Eastward Ho!*

Furthermore, as the incidents at Deptford receded into the past, there were fewer people interested in probing into the truth of the matter. No one in his lifetime seems to have credited Shakespeare of Stratford with any literary fame or talents and no one, eight years after his death, saw fit to deprive him of his borrowed glory.

If, as is likely, those in the know were sworn to secrecy, they would have felt constrained to keep their oaths indefinitely. One is reminded of Horatio and the soldiers on the battlements of Elsinore, who promised never to breathe a word about having seen the ghost of Hamlet's father. To take a modern parallel, staff employed at Bletchley Park and elsewhere in World War II, were sworn to secrecy and refused to talk about their work long after the war ended. If Marlowe's friends had likewise been sworn to secrecy, they would probably have felt obliged to carry the secret, of what happened at Deptford, to their graves. Their silence would have been even more absolute if, as has been suggested, there was a connection with the establishment of freemasonry.

The Civil War saw the closing of the theatres, after which the demand was for lighter and bawdier entertainment. It was 100 years before the actor David Garrick began the great adulation of the Bard. Generations of scholars thereafter devoted their lives to finding evidence to prove the genius of the man from Stratford, but all to no avail. Not a scrap of evidence has ever been discovered to prove that William Shakespeare (or Shaksper as he spelled his name) of Stratford wrote anything at all, apart from several signatures that suggest a lack of familiarity with writing his own name, and the excruciating verse that stands above his grave in Holy Trinity church, Stratford:

GOOD FREND FOR JESUS SAKE FORBEARE,
TO DIG THE DUST ENCLOASED HEARE,
BLESE BE YE MAN YT SPARES THES STONES
AND CURST BE HE YT MOVES MY BONES

Despite the lack of evidence to support the claims of Stratfordians, the name of William Shakespeare has become indelibly fixed in the imagination of the world as that of the greatest writer in the English language and possibly in the whole history of the world. Doubts have occasionally surfaced, as they did in the early nineteenth century, as the result of an explosive riposte to David Strauss's *Life of Jesus*, in which he took an agnostic view of the divinity of Christ. Samuel Mosheim Schmuker, a devout Christian, poured scorn on Strauss's view, saying that it would be as ridiculous to doubt the divinity of

Jesus as to doubt the authenticity of Shakespeare. Others were prompted to do precisely that, and proceeded to examine the evidence for what Schmuker derided as so ridiculous. They began to look more closely at the sacred name of Shakespeare, and they concluded that there was some reason to doubt its authenticity. Why the lack of evidence during his lifetime? Why the silence of his contemporaries at his death? Why the failure of his fellow citizens to take any notice of their fellow townsman? And why did he suddenly retreat to Stratford in the middle of writing a play about *Henry VIII*?

Questions abound as to the life and death of Marlowe: Who was 'the dark lady' of the sonnets? Where and when did he die, and how did he meet his end? But there is no logical inconsistency in admitting that we do not know, and every reason to search for evidence to corroborate the Marlovian hypothesis. Once again, Roe offers some useful clues as to where we might begin. Just a fraction of the resources expended by scholars on the pursuit of Shakespeare's humdrum life might considerably extend our knowledge of the true genius behind the works.

There is no lack of candidates to fill the place of the man from Stratford. Perhaps the strongest case is that made for the Earl of Oxford. Several other noblemen such as the Earl of Derby, the Earl of Rutland and, more recently, Sir Henry Neville, all have their supporters. The only female candidate seriously advanced as the true author is Mary Sidney, Countess of Pembroke. She was known to be the most educated woman in England, apart from the Queen, and she occupied the centre of the most important literary circle of the time. But neither Mary Sidney nor any of her male contenders stand close scrutiny. We might note also the case made for another noble contender in William Hastings, set out in the book, *Breaking the Shakespeare Codes*, by Robert Neild. It neatly answers all the questions posed by the shortcomings of other contenders, but it depends entirely on the evidence of cryptography, on messages buried in non-linear anagrams, mainly deduced from contemporary authors such as Ben Jonson and Francis Bacon. It would be wonderful to see Neild's research as the definitive answer to the Shakespearean riddle, but it depends almost entirely on cryptographic sleight of hand.

In the nineteenth century, an American lady, Delia Bacon, set out to demonstrate the case for her namesake, Francis Bacon, as the true author. Her cause was supported by others with even greater enthusiasm. Dr Owen claimed to have discovered a code, or cipher, by which he devised a whole saga of Elizabethan life and politics surrounding the Queen and her illegitimate son, Francis Bacon. It is a story told with salacious delight by Comyns Beaumont in *The Secret Life of the Virgin Queen*, published in 1947.

In 1901, in an attempt to prove the Baconian attribution, an appeal was made to a scientist, Dr Thomas Mendenhall, to subject samples of Shakespeare's writing for comparison with the work of Bacon and others. Mendenhall was a distinguished physicist and President of the American Association for the Advancement of Science, who had developed a method of telling different authors by their use of words of different length. He made a careful analysis of several thousand words from each of the writers, recording the frequency with which they used words of two, three or four letters or more. Every writer consciously or unconsciously tends to conform to a particular pattern. The result of Mendenhall's test showed no consistency between Bacon and Shakespeare, or any other writer except Christopher Marlowe, for whom there was a perfect match with Shakespeare (see Figure 1). It is perhaps dangerous to draw too many conclusions from word-length patterns alone, but Mendenhall's experiments have been replicated by modern scholars with identical results (see Daryl Pinksen, *Marlowe's Ghost*, 52–61).

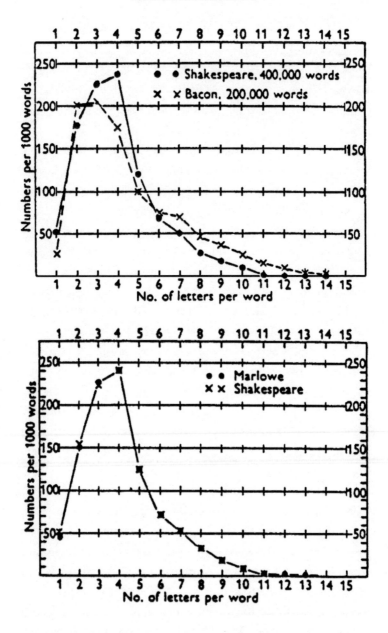

Figure 1 Mendenhall's graphs showing no close convergence in word-length patterns of Bacon and Shakespeare, but an almost perfect match for Shakespeare and Marlowe.

Reproduced from A.D. Wraight, *The Story that the Sonnets Tell*, 315, 317.

Stylistic analysis is notoriously subjective, and it is difficult to rid one's mind of the notion that Shakespeare and Marlowe were two different writers with their own peculiar approach to dramatic writing. Devotees of Shakespeare assert that Marlowe has none of the breadth and depth of understanding that is found in Shakespeare, but is that not understandable in view of the human tragedy that befell Marlowe in the interim between his former life and that of Shakespeare, the exile? To lose one's reputation, one's family and friends and to be condemned to a life in exile was bound to deepen the understanding and sensibilities of the younger man. So many of his great characters, like Hamlet and Lear, echo his own reversal of fortune. In depicting them and their tragic fate he was drawing upon his own depths of despair.

It is often said that Marlowe lacked Shakespeare's comic genius, but this is hard to square with the comic relief afforded by minor characters such as Wagner in *Dr Faustus*. Many actors will assert that playing Marlowe is a different experience from that gained in performing Shakespeare, and our devotion to the Bard makes us resist any idea that Marlowe and Shakespeare are one and the same. I have sometimes tested this conviction by proffering a 'Stork and butter' test – asking people to say whether a variety of quotations are from Marlowe or Shakespeare. The results suggest that few people can detect a difference.

A great many literary authorities have had to admit that Shakespeare owed a huge debt to his precursor. Pinksen gives many examples of expert opinion which stress the close similarity of the two writers. In 1886, A.C. Verity wrote a book entitled *The Influence of Christopher Marlowe on Shakespeare's*

Earlier Style. He averred that: 'Blank verse, as we understand it, came into birth at the bidding of Christopher Marlowe.' In 1946, Charles Norman in *Christopher Marlowe: The Muse's Darling*, wrote that the play *Edward II* 'shows how Marlowe, if he had lived, would have matured; this is the book with which Shakespeare went to school. Only five years had elapsed since *Tamburlaine*, but there is here a development as impressive as Shakespeare's was to be – perhaps it was more impressive'.

In 1934, Parrott, in *William Shakespeare: A Handbook*, wrote: 'Without Marlowe, there would never have been the William Shakespeare whom we know.' More recently, A.L. Rowse, in *Shakespeare: The Man* (1973), wrote that 'Marlowe's historic achievement was to marry great poetry to the drama; his was the originating genius. William Shakespeare never forgot him; in his penultimate valedictory play, *The Tempest*, he is still echoing Marlowe's phrases.' 'Shakespeare', says Jonathan Bate, in *The Genius of Shakespeare* (1997), 'only became Shakespeare because of the death of Marlowe. And he remained peculiarly haunted by that death'. In 2004, Stephen Greenblatt, in his book *Will in the World: How Shakespeare Became Shakespeare* declared that 'The fingerprints of *Tamburlaine* are all over the plays that are among Shakespeare's earliest known ventures as a playwright.'

There is, of course, a myriad of writers who affirm, as an article of faith, that the two men are quite different in style of writing and who have unquestioning faith in the man from Stratford. Recent support for this view comes in a compilation of expert views collected together by the Shakespeare Birthplace Trust, entitled *Shakespeare Beyond Doubt* (2013). However, it does not amount to anything more than a chorus of affirmation rather than offering any evidence in support of the argument. There are no actual facts to link the man from Stratford to the writing of the plays. Mark Twain, in his 'Is

Shakespeare Dead?', ridiculed his credentials, pointing to the silence that marked his passing:

> 'When Shakespeare died in Stratford *it was not an event*. It made no more stir in England than the death of any other forgotten theatre-actor would have made. Nobody came down from London; there were no lamenting poems, no eulogies, no national tears – there was merely silence, and nothing more. A striking contrast with what happened when Ben Jonson, and Francis Bacon, and Spenser, and Raleigh and other distinguished literary folk of Shakespeare's time passed from life! No praiseful voice was lifted for the lost Bard of Avon; even Ben Jonson waited seven years before he lifted his. *So far as anybody actually knows and can prove*, Shakespeare of Stratford-on-Avon never wrote a play in his life.'

Another American, Henry James, wrote that he was "'a sort of' haunted by the conviction that the divine William is the biggest and most successful fraud ever practised on a patient world. The more I turn him round and round the more he so affects me" (letter to Violet Hunt, 26 August 1903, quoted in James Shapiro, *Contested Will*, 165).

Germaine Greer acknowledged in her book, *Shakespeare's Wife* (2007) that: 'All biographies of Shakespeare are houses built of straw.' There is just nothing to go on but the rather mundane references to legal disputes with his neighbours and records pertaining to his father's business, purchases of land and property, etc., nothing whatever to link him to the life of England's foremost poet. The authors of another recent study of Shakespeare, Emma Jones and Rhiannon Guy, in *The Shakespeare Companion* (2005), say: 'the hard facts we know about Shakespeare do not amount to much more than a rhyming couplet'. As Mark Twain pointed out, the only poem he claimed to have written was the excruciating doggerel in St Mary's church at Stratford. William Shakespeare just cannot be made to fit the profile of the erudite, perspicacious, much-travelled man who gave us a cornucopia of poems and plays that have fascinated and entertained the world ever since.

It may be argued that it matters not who wrote the plays and poetry attributed to William Shakespeare, but I would assert that it does indeed matter. It matters because we always seek to know the minds of men and women who enrich our own lives by their creative imagination. It matters because the truth always matters, and if we have been singing the praises of the wrong man for 400 years, it is high time we did honour to the rightful genius. It matters because by attributing the sublime works to a man of no known education and no access to great libraries or higher learning, we give support to the cult of the mediocre – to the notion that one does not need a university education or great scholarship to produce works of great depth and quality. It may even be that this contributes to the Englishman's refusal to learn foreign languages, since Shakespeare apparently picked up enough Spanish, French, Italian, as well as Greek and Latin, without apparently ever leaving England or learning to speak anything but English.

It matters too, because if the works of Marlowe are seen as part of the Shakespearean canon, a whole new world of scholarship is opened up. Think of the scope for research into the records of contemporary Italy, pursuing, among other things, the riddle of his death – when and where did it happen? And think of the wealth of new material for programme notes. I think it also affects our view of the social mores of the time.

If William Shakespeare of Stratford really did write the plays and poetry attributed to him, then historians will tend to see the social context of his life as one affording a degree of freedom to writers to speak their minds without fear, since no one ever attempted to muzzle Shakespeare, let alone throw him into jail for heresy or treason.

Our view of educational opportunities may also be falsely coloured by the notion that a poor lad, from a market town in Warwickshire, could self-educate to the extent that Shakespeare would have had to. Our whole view of Elizabethan England is coloured by our conception of the life and milieu of the man from Stratford. However, if we were to concentrate on the real-life experiences of Marlowe, then the petty-mindedness of the Church and the machinations of Burghley in protecting Marlowe would open up an entire reinterpretation of life in Elizabethan England.

Abroad, too, it would give impetus to closer study and perhaps to a clearer picture of the truth about Marlowe's experiences in France and Italy. When shall we see cultural tours to Marlowe's Mediterranean? Italy surely has as much right to claim Shakespeare as the English have to claim Handel or Nicholas Pevsner as belonging to them.

There would have to be changes at Stratford, but the town has so much more to attract visitors than bardolatry, and it will always be a magnet for tourists, seeking some appreciation of the world that produced the literary output attributed to William. The conundrum posed by Alice Hamilton, as to how two men of preternatural genius emerged in England at the very same time, is satisfactorily resolved if we accept the overwhelming evidence showing them to have been one and the same. Maybe we should just refer to them in future as 'Christopher Shakespeare'.

Index

ℓ